COMPARATIVE STUDIES
IN NURSERY RHYMES

COMPARATIVE STUDIES
IN
NURSERY RHYMES

BY

LINA ECKENSTEIN
AUTHOR OF " WOMAN UNDER MONASTICISM "

There were more things in Mrs. Gurton's eye,
Mayhap, than are dreamed of in our philosophy
C. S. CALVERLEY

LONDON
DUCKWORTH & CO.
1906
Now Reissued by
Singing Tree Press
1249 Washington Blvd., Detroit, Michigan 1968

First published 1906

Library of Congress Catalog Card Number 68–23469

TO THE GENTLE READER

THE walls of the temple of King Sety at
Abydos in Upper Egypt are decorated
with sculptured scenes which represent the cult
of the gods and the offerings brought to them.
In a side chapel there is depicted the following
curious scene. A dead figure lies extended on a
bier; sorrowing hawks surround him; a flying
hawk reaches down a seal amulet from above.
Had I succeeded in procuring a picture of the
scene, it would stand reproduced here; for the
figure and his mourners recalled the quaint little
woodcut of a toy-book which told the tale of
the Death and Burial of Cock Robin. The sculp-
tures of Sety date from the fourteenth century
before Christ; the knell of the robin can be traced
back no further than the middle of the eighteenth
century A.D. Can the space that lies between be
bridged over, and the conception of the dead robin

be linked on to that of the dead hawk ? However that may be, the sight of the sculptured scene strengthened my resolve to place some of the coincidences of comparative nursery lore before the gentle reader. It lies with him to decide whether the wares are such as to make a further instalment desirable.

23 *September*, 1906.

CONTENTS

. . . To my gaze the phantoms of the Past,
The cherished fictions of my boyhood, rise:

 · · · · · ·

The House that Jack built—and the Malt that lay
Within the House—the Rat that ate the Malt—
The Cat, that in that sanguinary way
Punished the poor thing for its venial fault—
The Worrier-Dog—the Cow with crumpled horn—
And then—ah yes! and then—the Maiden all forlorn!

O Mrs. Gurton—(may I call thee Gammer?)
Thou more than mother to my infant mind!
I loved thee better than I loved my grammar—
I used to wonder why the Mice were blind,
And who was gardener to Mistress Mary,
And what—I don't know still—was meant by "quite
  contrary."   C. S. C.

  The dates that stand after the separate rhymes refer to the list of
English collections on p. 11 ; the capital letters in brackets refer to
the list of books on p. 221.

COMPARATIVE STUDIES
IN NURSERY RHYMES

CHAPTER I

FIRST APPEARANCE OF RHYMES
IN PRINT

THE study of folk-lore has given a new interest to much that seemed insignificant and trivial. Among the unheeded possessions of the past that have gained a fresh value are nursery rhymes. A nursery rhyme I take to be a rhyme that was passed on by word of mouth and taught to children before it was set down in writing and put into print. The use of the term in this application goes back to the early part of the nineteenth century. In 1834 John Gawler, afterwards Bellenden Ker, published the first volume of his *Essay on the Archaiology of*

Popular English Phrases and Nursery Rhymes, a fanciful production.   Prior to this time nursery rhymes were usually spoken of as nursery songs.

The interest in these "unappreciated trifles of the nursery," as Rimbault called them, was aroused towards the close of the eighteenth century.   In a letter which Joseph Ritson wrote to his little nephew, he mentioned the collection of rhymes known as *Mother Goose's Melody*, and assured him that he also would set about collecting rhymes.[1]   His collection of rhymes is said, in the *Dictionary of National Biography*, to have been published at Stockton in 1783 under the title *Gammer Gurton's Garland*.   A copy of an anonymous collection of rhymes published by Christopher and Jennett at Stockton, which is called *Gammer Gurton's Garland or the Nursery Parnassus*, is now at the British Museum, and is designated as a "new edition with additions."   It bears no name and no date, but its contents, which consist of over seventy rhymes, agree with parts 1 and 2 of a large collection of nursery rhymes,

---

[1] *Letters of Joseph Ritson*, edited by his Nephew, 1833. 27 April, 1781.

including over one hundred and forty pieces, which were published in 1810 by the publisher R. Triphook, of 37 St. James Street, London, who also issued other collections made by Ritson.

The collection of rhymes known as *Mother Goose's Melody*, which aroused the interest of Ritson, was probably the toy-book which was entered for copyright in London on 28 December, 1780. Its title was *Mother Goose's Melody or Sonnets for the Cradle*, and it was entered by John Carnan, the stepson of the famous publisher John Newbery, who had succeeded to the business in partnership with Francis Newbery.[1] Of this book no copy is known to exist. Toy-books, owing to the careless way in which they are handled, are amongst the most perishable literature. Many toy-books are known to have been issued in hundreds of copies, yet of some of these not a single copy can now be traced.

The name Mother Goose, its connection with nursery rhymes, and the date of issue of *Mother Goose's Melody*, have been the subject of some

[1] Welsh, Ch., *A Publisher of the Last Century*, 1885, p. 272.

4 COMPARATIVE STUDIES

contention. Thomas Fleet, a well-known printer
of Boston, Mass., who was from Shropshire, is
said to have issued a collection of nursery rhymes
under the following title, *Songs for the Nursery,
or Mother Goose's Melodies for Children*, printed
by Thomas Fleet at his printing-house, Pudding
Lane, 1719, price two coppers.[1] The existence
of this book at the date mentioned has been both
affirmed and denied.[2] John Fleet Eliot, a great-
grandson of the printer, accepted its existence, and
in 1834 wrote with regard to it as follows: "It is
well known to antiquaries that more than a hundred years ago there was a small book in circulation
in London bearing the name of *Rhymes for the
Nursery or Lulla-Byes for Children*, which contained many of the identical pieces of *Mother
Goose's Melodies* of the present day. It contained also other pieces, more silly if possible,
and some that the American types of the present
day would refuse to give off an impression. The
cuts or illustrations thereof were of the coarsest

[1] Appleton, *Cyclopædia of American Biography*, 1887 :
Fleet, Thomas.
[2] Whitmore, W. H., *The original Mother Goose's Melody*,
1892, p. 40 ff.

description." On the other hand, the date of 1719 in connection with the expression "two coppers," has been declared impossible. However this may be, no copy of the book of Fleet or of its presumed prototype has been traced.

The name Mother Goose, which John Newbery and others associated with nursery rhymes, may have been brought into England from France, where *La Mère Oie* was connected with the telling of fairy tales as far back as 1650.[1] *La Mère Oie* is probably a lineal descendant of *La Reine Pédauque*, otherwise *Berthe au grand pied*, but there is the possibility also of the relationship to *Fru Gode* or *Fru Gosen* of German folklore. We first come across Mother Goose in England in connection with the famous puppet-showman Robert Powell, who set up his show in Bath and in Covent Garden, London, between 1709 and 1711. The repertory of his plays, which were of his own composing, included *Whittington and his Cat, The Children in the Wood, Friar Bacon and Friar Bungay, Robin Hood and Little*

[1] Lang, A., *Perrault's Popular Tales*, 1888. Introduction, XXIV.

John, Mother Shipton, and *Mother Goose.*[1] A play or pantomime called *Mother Goose* was still popular at the beginning of the nineteenth century, for the actor Grimaldi obtained his greatest success in it in 1806.[2]

The name Gammer Gurton which Ritson chose for his collection of rhymes, was traditional also. *Gammer Gurton's Needle* is the name of a famous old comedy which dates from about the year 1566. The name also appears in connection with nursery rhymes in a little toy-book, issued by Lumsden in Glasgow, which is called *Gammer Gurton's Garland of Nursery Songs, and Toby Tickle's Collection of Riddles.* This is undated. It occurs also in an insignificant little toy-book called *The Topbook of all,* in connection with Nurse Lovechild, Jacky Nory, and Tommy Thumb. This book is also undated, but contains the picture of a shilling of 1760 which is referred to as "a new shilling."

The date at which nursery rhymes appeared in

---

[1] Collier, J. P., *Punch and Judy, citing "A Second Tale of a Tub or the History of Robert Powell, the puppet-show-man, 1715."*

[2] *Dictionary of National Biography,* Grimaldi.

print yields one clue to their currency at a given period. The oldest dated collection of rhymes which I have seen bears the title *Tommy Thumb's Pretty Song Book*, vol. II, "sold by M. Cooper according to Act of Parliament." It is printed partly in red, partly in black, and on its last page bears the date 1744. A copy of this is at the British Museum.

Next to this in date is a toy-book which is called *The Famous Tommy Thumb's Little Story-Book*, printed and sold at the printing office in Marlborough Street, 1771. A copy of this is in the library of Boston, Mass. It contains nine nursery rhymes at the end, which have been reprinted by Whitmore.

Other collections of rhymes issued in America have been preserved which are reprints of earlier English collections. Among these is *Tommy Thumb's Song Book for all Little Masters and Misses*, by Nurse Lovechild, which is dated 1788, and was printed by Isaiah Thomas at Worcester, Mass. A copy is at the British Museum.

Isaiah Thomas was in direct connection with England, where he procured, in 1786, the first fount of music type that was carried to America. Among many toy-books of his that are reprints from English publications, he issued *Mother Goose's Melody, Sonnets for the Cradle.* A copy of this book which is designated as the third Worcester edition, bears the date 1799, and has been reprinted in facsimile by Whitmore. It was probably identical with the collection of rhymes for which the firm of Newberry received copyright in 1780, and which was mentioned by Ritson. Other copies of *Mother Goose's Melody,* one bearing the watermark of 1803, and the other issued by the firm of John Marshall, which is undated, are now at the Bodleian.[1] Thus the name of Mother Goose was largely used in connection with nursery rhymes.

The second half of the eighteenth century witnessed a great development in toy-book literature. The leader of the movement was John Newbery, a man of considerable attainments, who sold drugs and literature, and who came from Reading to London in 1744, and settled in St. Paul's Churchyard, where his establishment

[1] Whitmore, loc. cit., p. 6.

became a famous centre of the book trade. Among those whom he had in his employ were Griffith Jones (d. 1786) and Oliver Goldsmith (d. 1774), whose versatility and delicate humour gave a peculiar charm to the books for children which they helped to produce.

In London Newbery had a rival in John Marshall, whose shop in Aldermary Churchyard was known already in 1787 as the *Great A, and Bouncing B Toy Factory*. This name was derived from a current nursery rhyme on the alphabet, which occurs as follows:—

> Great A, little a, Bouncing B,
> The cat's in the cupboard, and she can't see.
> (1744, p. 22.)

A number of provincial publishers followed their example. Among them were Thomas Saint, in Newcastle, who between 1771 and 1774 employed the brothers Bewick ; Kendrew, in York ; Lumsden, in Glasgow ; Drewey, in Derby ; Rusher, in Banbury ; and others. The toy-books that were issued by these firms have much likeness to one another, and are often illustrated by the same cuts. Most of them are undated.

Among the books issued by Rusher were *Nursery Rhymes from the Royal Collections*, and *Nursery Poems from the Ancient and Modern Poets*, which contain some familiar rhymes in versions which differ from those found elsewhere.

Besides these toy-book collections, there is a large edition of *Gammer Gurton's Garland*, of the year 1810, which contains the collections of 1783 with considerable additions. In the year 1826, Chambers published his *Popular Rhymes of Scotland*, which contained some fireside stories and nursery rhymes, the number of which was considerably increased in the enlarged edition of 1870. In the year 1842, Halliwell, under the auspices of the Percy Society, issued the *Nursery Rhymes of England*, which were reprinted in 1843, and again in an enlarged edition in 1846. Three years later he supplemented this book by a collection of *Popular Rhymes* which contain many traditional game rhymes and many valuable remarks and criticisms.

These books, together with the rhymes of Gawler, and a collection of *Old Nursery Rhymes with Tunes*, issued by Rimbault in 1864, exhaust

the collections of nursery rhymes which have
a claim on the attention of the student. Most
of their contents were subsequently collected and
issued by the firm of Warne & Co., under the
title *Mother Goose's Nursery Rhymes, Tales and
Jingles*, of which the issue of 1890 contains over
seven hundred pieces. In the list which follows,
I have arranged these various collections of rhymes
in the order of their issue, with a few modern
collections that contain further rhymes. Of those
which are bracketed I have not succeeded in finding a copy.

(1719. *Songs for the Nursery, or Mother Goose's
Melodies.* Printed by T. Fleet.)

1744. *Tommy Thumb's Pretty Song Book.*

c. 1760. *The Topbook of all.*

(1771. *Tommy Thumb's Little Story Book.* The nine
rhymes which this contains are cited by Whitmore.)

(1780. *Mother Goose's Melody,* for which copyright was
taken by John Carnan.)

c. 1783. *Gammer Gurton's Garland.*

1788. *Tommy Thumb's Song Book,* issued by Isaiah
Thomas.

(1797. *Infant Institutes,* cited by Halliwell and Rimbault.)

1799. *Mother Goose's Melody.* Facsimile reprint by
Whitmore.

1810. *Gammer Gurton's Garland.* The enlarged edition, published by R. Triphook, 37 St. James Street, London.

1826. Chambers, *Popular Rhymes of Scotland.*

1834–9. Ker, *Essays on the Archaiology of Nursery Rhymes.*

1842–3. Halliwell, *The Nursery Rhymes of England.*

1846. Halliwell, ditto. Enlarged and annotated edition.

1849. Halliwell, *Popular Rhymes.*

1864. Rimbault, *Old Nursery Rhymes with tunes.*

1870. Chambers, *Popular Rhymes of Scotland.* Enlarged edition.

1876. Thiselton Dyer, *British Popular Customs.*

ˊ1890. *Mother Goose's Nursery Rhymes, Tales and Jingles.* Issued by Warne & Co.

1892. Northall, G. F., *English Folk Rhymes.*

1894. Gomme, A. B., *The Traditional Games of England, Scotland, and Ireland.*

In the studies which follow, the rhymes cited have attached to them the date of the collection in which they occur.

CHAPTER II

EARLY REFERENCES

INDEPENDENTLY of these collections of nursery rhymes, many rhymes are cited in general literature. This yields a further clue to their currency at a given period. Thus Rimbault describes a book called *Infant Institutes, part the first, or a Nurserical Essay on the Poetry Lyric and Allegorical of the Earliest Ages,* 1797, perhaps by B. N. Turner, the friend of Dr. Johnson, which was intended to ridicule the Shakespeare commentators (*N. & Q.,* 5, 3, 441). In the course of his argument, the author cites a number of nursery rhymes.

Again, the poet Henry Carey, about the year 1720, ridiculed the odes addressed to children by Ambrose Philips by likening these to a jumble of nursery rhymes. In doing so he cited the rhymes, "Namby Pamby Jack a Dandy," "Lon-

don Bridge is broken down," " Liar Lickspit,"
"Jacky Horner," "See-saw," and others, which
nowadays are still included among the ordinary
stock of our rhymes.

Again, in the year 1671, John Eachard, the
divine, illustrated his argument by quoting the
alphabet rhyme "A was an apple pie," as far as
" G got it."[1] Instances such as these do not, however, carry us back farther than the seventeenth
century.

Another clue to the date of certain rhymes is
afforded by their mention of historical persons,
in a manner which shows that the rhyme in this
form was current at the time when the individual
whom they mention was prominently before the
eyes of the public.   Halliwell recorded from oral
tradition the following verse :—

> Doctor Sacheverel
> Did very well,
> But Jacky Dawbin
> Gave him a warning.   (1849, p. 12.)

The verse refers to Dr. Sacheverel, the noncon-
formist minister who preached violent sermons in

[1] Eachard, *Observations, etc.*, 1671, cited.   Halliwell,
Popular Rhymes, 1849, p. 137.

St. Paul's, pointing at the Whig members as false friends and real enemies of the Church. John Dolben (1662–1710) called attention to them in the House of Commons, and they were declared "malicious, scandalous, and seditious libels."

Again there is the rhyme :—

> Lucy Locket lost her pocket,
> Kitty Fisher found it,
> But the devil a penny was there in it,
> Except the binding round it.   (1849, p. 48.)

This is said to preserve the names of two celebrated courtesans of the reign of Charles II (1892, p. 330).

The first name in the following rhyme is that of a famous border hero who was hanged between 1529 and 1530 :—

> Johnny Armstrong killed a calf;
> Peter Henderson got half;
> Willy Wilkinson got the head,—
> Ring the bell, the calf is dead.
>   (1890, p. 358.)

Among the pieces collected by Halliwell, and told in cumulative form, one begins and ends with the following line, which recurs at the end of every verse :—

> John Ball shot them all.

Halliwell is of opinion that this may refer to the priest who took a prominent part in the rebellion at the time of Richard II, and who was hanged, drawn, and quartered in 1381.

But a historical name does not necessarily indicate the date of a rhyme. For a popular name is sometimes substituted for one that has fallen into contempt or obscurity. Moreover, a name may originally have indicated a person other than the one with whom it has come to be associated.

A familiar nursery song printed in the collection of *c.* 1783, and extant in several variants, is as follows :—

> When good King Arthur rul'd the land,
> He was a goodly king,
> He stole three pecks of barley meal
> To make a bag pudding.
> A bag pudding the king did make
> And stuff'd it well with plumbs,
> And in it put great lumps of fat,
> As big as my two thumbs.
> The king and queen did eat thereof,
> And noblemen beside,
> And what they could not eat that night
> The queen next morning fry'd. (*c.* 1783, p. 32.)

Mr. Chappell, as cited by Halliwell, considered

that this version is not the correct one, but the
one which begins :—

> King Stephen was a worthy king
> As ancient bards do sing . . . .

The same story related in one verse only, and
in simpler form, connects it with Queen Elizabeth,
in a version recovered in Berkshire.

> Our good Quane Bess, she maayde a pudden,
> An stuffed un well o' plumes ;
> And in she put gurt dabs o' vat,
> As big as my two thumbs.   (1892, p. 289.)

On the face of it the last variant appears to be
the oldest.

An interesting example of a change of name,
and of the changing meaning of a name, is
afforded by the nursery song that is told of
King Arthur, and *mutatis mutandis* of Old King
Cole.   The poem of King Arthur is as follows:—

> When Arthur first in Court began
> To wear long hanging sleeves,
> He entertained three serving men
> And all of them were thieves.
>
> The first he was an Irishman,
> The second was a Scot,
> The third he was a Welshman,
> And all were knaves, I wot.

c

The Irishman loved usquebaugh,
The Scot loved ale called blue-cap.
The Welshman he loved toasted cheese,
And made his mouth like a mouse-trap.

Usquebaugh burnt the Irishman,
The Scot was drowned in ale,
The Welshman had liked to be choked by a mouse,
But he pulled it out by the tail.

In this form the piece is designated as a glee, and is printed in the *New Lyric* by Badcock of about 1720, which contains "the best songs now in vogue."

In the nursery collection of Halliwell of 1842 there is a parallel piece to this which stands as follows :—

Old King Cole was a merry old soul
And a merry old soul was he ;
Old King Cole he sat in his hole,
And he called for his fiddlers three.

The first he was a miller,
The second he was a weaver,
The third he was a tailor,
And all were rogues together.

The miller he stole corn,
The weaver he stole yarn,
The little tailor stole broadcloth
To keep these three rogues warm.

The miller was drowned in his dam,
The weaver was hung in his loom,
The devil ran away with the little tailor
With the broadcloth under his arm.

(1842, p. 3.)

Chappell printed the words of the song of Old King Cole in several variations, and pointed out that *The Pleasant Historie of Thomas of Reading, or the Six Worthie Yeomen of the West* of 1632, contains the legend of one Cole, a cloth-maker of Reading at the time of King Henry I, and that the name " became proverbial owing to the popularity of this book." " There was some joke or conventional meaning among Elizabethan dramatists," he says, " when they gave the name of Old Cole, which it is now difficult to recover." Dekker in the *Satiromatrix* of 1602, and Marston in *The Malcontent* of 1604, applied the name to a woman. On the other hand, Ben Jonson in *Bartholomew Fair* gave the name of Old Cole to the sculler in the puppet-play *Hero and Leander* which he there introduces.[1] In face of this information, what becomes of the identity of the supposed king ?

[1] Chappell, *Popular Music of the Olden Time*, 1893, p. 633.

On the other hand a long ancestry is now claimed for certain characters of nursery fame who seemed to have no special claim to attention. The following verse appears in most collections of rhymes, and judging from the illustration which accompanies it in the toy-books, it refers some-times to a boy and a girl, sometimes to two boys.

> Jack and Gill went up the hill
> To fetch a bottle of water ;
> Jack fell down and broke his crown,
> And Gill came tumbling after.

(*c.* 1783, p. 51.)

[Later collections have *Jill* and *pail.*]

This verse, as was first suggested by Baring-Gould,[1] preserves the Scandinavian myth of the children Hjuki and Bill who were caught up by Mani, the Moon, as they were taking water from the well Byrgir, and they can be seen to this day in the moon carrying the bucket on the pole between them.

Another rhyme cited by Halliwell from *The New Mad Tom o' Bedlam* mentions Jack as being the Man in the Moon :—

[1] Baring-Gould, *Curious Myths of the Middle Ages*, 1866, p. 189.

The Man in the Moon drinks claret,
But he is a dull Jack-a-dandy ;
Would he know a sheep's head from a carrot,
He should learn to drink cider or brandy.

(1842, p. 33.)

According to North German belief, a man
stands in the moon pouring water out of a pail
(K., p. 304), which agrees with expressions such as
" the moon holds water." In a Norse mnemonic
verse which dates from before the twelfth century, we read, " the pail is called Saeg, the
pole is called Simul, Bil and Hiuk carry them "
(C. P., I, 78).

The view that Jack and Jill are mythological
or heroic beings finds corroboration in the expression " for Jak nor for Gille," which occurs in
the Townley Mysteries of about the year 1460.[1]
By this declaration a superhuman power is called
in as witness. The same names are coupled
together also in an ancient divination rhyme used
to decide in favour of one of two courses of
action. Two scraps of paper slightly moistened
were placed on the back of the hand, and the
following invocation was pronounced before and

[2] Cited *Murray's Dictionary:* Jack.

after breathing upon them to see which would fly first. The sport was taught by Goldsmith to Miss Hawkins when a child, as she related to Forster.[1]

> There were two blackbirds sat upon a hill
> The one was named Jack, the other named Jill.
> Fly away Jack ! Fly away Jill !
> Come again Jack ! Come again Jill ! (1810, p. 45.)

The lines suggest the augur's action with regard to the flight of birds. The same verse has been recited to me in the following variation :—

> Peter and Paul sat on the wall,
> Fly away Peter ! Fly away Paul !
> Come again Peter ! Come again Paul !

In this case the names of Christian apostles have been substituted for heathen names which, at the time when the *names* were changed, may still have carried a suggestion of profanity. The following rhyme on Jack and Gill occurs in an early nursery collection :—

> I won't be my father's Jack,
> I won't be my mother's Gill,
> I will be the fiddler's wife
> And have music when I will.
> T'other little tune, t'other little tune,
> Pr'ythee, love, play me, t'other little tune.
> (c. 1783, p. 25.)

[1] Forster, J., *Life of Goldsmith*, II, p. 71.

CHAPTER III

RHYMES AND POPULAR SONGS

ON looking more closely at the contents of
our nursery collections, we find that a large
proportion of so-called nursery rhymes are songs
or snatches of songs, which are preserved also as
broadsides, or appeared in printed form in early
song-books. These songs or parts of songs were
included in nursery collections because they happened to be current at the time when these
collections were made, and later compilers transferred into their own collections what they found
in earlier ones. Many songs are preserved in a
number of variations, for popular songs are in
a continual state of transformation. Sometimes
new words are written to the old tune, and
differ from those that have gone before in all but
the rhyming words at the end of the lines; sometimes new words are introduced which entirely

change the old meaning. Many variations of songs are born of the moment, and would pass away with it, were it not that they happen to be put into writing and thereby escape falling into oblivion.

In *Mother Goose's Melody* stands a song in six verses which begins :—

> There was a little man who woo'd a little maid,
> And he said : "Little maid, will you wed, wed, wed?
> I have little more to say, will you? Aye or nay?
> For little said is soonest mended, ded, ded."
>
> (1799, p. 46.)

Halliwell's collection includes only the first and the fourth verse of this piece. (1842, p. 24.)

In the estimation of Chappell this song was a very popular ballad, which was sung to the tune of *I am the Duke of Norfolk*, or *Paul's Steeple*.[1] It appears also in the *Fairing or Golden Toy for Children of all Sizes and Denominations* of 1781, where it is designated as "a new love song by the poets of Great Britain." Its words form a variation of the song called *The Dumb Maid*, which is extant in a broadside of about

---

[1] Chappell, loc. cit., p. 770.

1678,[1] and which is also included in the early
collection of *Pills to Purge Melancholy* of 1698–
1719. The likeness between the pieces depends
on their peculiar repeat :—

> There was a bonny blade had married a country maid,
> And safely conducted her home, home, home ;
> She was neat in every part, and she pleased him to the
>   heart, '
> But alas, and alas, she was dumb, dumb, dumb.

The same form of verse was used in another
nursery song which stands as follows :—

> There was a little man, and he had a little gun,
> And the ball was made of lead, lead, lead.
> And he went to a brook to shoot at a duck,
> And he hit her upon the head, head, head.

> Then he went home unto his wife Joan,
> To bid her a good fire to make, make, make,
> To roast the duck that swam in the brook,
> And he would go fetch her the drake, drake, drake.
>
> (1744, p. 43 ; with repeat, 1810, p. 45.)

Again, a song which appears in several early
nursery collections is as follows :—

> There was an old woman toss'd in a blanket,
> Seventeen times as high as the moon ;
> But where she was going no mortal could tell,
> For under her arm she carried a broom.

[1] *Roxburgh Collection of Ballads*, **IV**, p. 355.

"Old woman, old woman, old woman," said I,
"Whither, ah whither, ah whither, so high?"
To sweep the cobwebs from the sky,
And I'll be with you by and by.   (*c.* 1783, p. 22.)

This song was a favourite with Goldsmith, who sang it to his friends at dinner on the day when his play *The Good-natured Man* was produced.[1] It was one of the numerous songs that were sung to the tune of Lilliburlero, which goes back at least to the time of Purcell.[2] A Scottish version of this piece was printed by Chambers, which presents some interesting variations:—

There was a wee wifie row't up in a blanket,
Nineteen times as hie as the moon;
And what did she there I canna declare,
For in her oxter she bure the sun.
"Wee wifie, wee wifie, wee wifie," quo' I,
"O what are ye doin' up there sae hie?"
"I'm blowin' the cauld cluds out o' the sky."
"Weel dune, weel dune, wee wifie!" quo' I.

                     (1870, p. 34.)

I have come across a verse sung on Earl Grey and Lord Brougham, written in 1835, which may have been in imitation of this song:—

[1] Forster, *Life of Goldsmith*, II, 122.
[2] Chappell, loc. cit., p. 569.

Mother Bunch shall we visit the moon?
Come, mount on your broom, I'll stick on a spoon,
Then hey to go, we shall be there soon . . . etc.

Mother Bunch is a familiar character of British folk-lore, who figures in old chapbooks as a keeper of old-world saws, and gives advice in matters matrimonial. One of the earliest accounts of her is *Pasquill's Jests with the Merriments of Mother Bunch*, extant in several editions, which was reprinted by Hazlitt in *Old English Jestbooks*, 1864, Vol. III. There are also *Mother Bunch's Closet newly broke open*, *Mother Bunch's Golden Fortune Teller*, and *Mother Bunch's Fairy Tales*, published by Harris in 1802. The name also occurs in *Mother Osborne's Letter to the Protestant Dissenters rendered into English Metre by Mother Bunch*, 1733. Mother Bunch, like Mother Goose and Mother Shipton, may be a traditional name, for Mother Bunch has survived in connections which suggest both the wise woman and the witch.

Another old song which figures in early nursery collections is as follows :—

What care I how black I be?
Twenty pounds will marry me ;
If twenty won't, forty shall—
I am my mother's bouncing girl.
(c. 1783, p. 57.)

Chappell mentions a song called, *What care I how fair she be*, which goes back to before 1620.[1] The words of these songs seem to have suggested a parody addressed to Zachary Macaulay, the father of the historian, who pleaded the cause of the slaves. The Bill for the abolition of slavery was passed in 1833, and the following quatrain was sung with reference to it :—

What though now opposed I be?
Twenty peers will carry me.
If twenty won't, thirty will,
For I'm His Majesty's bouncing Bill.
(*N. & Q.*, 8, XII, 48.)

Another so-called nursery rhyme which is no more than a popular song has been traced some way back in history by Halliwell, who gives it in two variations :—

Three blind mice, see how they run !
They all run after the farmer's wife,
Who cut off their tails with a carving knife,
Did you ever see such fools in your life—
Three blind mice !   (1846, p. 5.)

---

[1] Chappell, loc. cit., p. 315.

In *Deuteromalia* of 1609 this stands as follows :—

> Three blind mice, three blind mice !
> Dame Julian, the miller and his merry old wife
> She scrapte the tripe, take thow the knife.

Among the popular songs which have found their way into nursery collections is the one known as *A Frog he would a wooing go*, the subject of which is old. Already in 1549 the shepherds of Scotland sang a song called, *The Frog cam to the Myldur*. In the year 1580 there was licensed, *A most strange Wedding of the Frog and the Mouse*, as appears from the books of the Stationers' Company cited by Warton.[1] The song has been preserved in many variations with a variety of burdens. These burdens sound like nonsense, but in some cases the same words appear elsewhere in a different application, which shows that they were not originally unmeaning.

The oldest known version of the song begins :—

> It was a frog in the well, *humble dum, humble dum,*
> And the mouse in the mill, *tweedle tweedle twino.*[2]

[1] Warton, *History of English Poetry*, 1840, III, 360.
[2] Chappell, loc. cit., p. 88.

The expression *humble dum* occurs in other songs and seems to indicate triumph; the word *tweedle* represents the sound made by the pipes.

A Scottish variation of the song begins :—

> There lived a Puddy in a well, *Cuddy alone, Cuddy alone,*
> There lived a Puddy in a well, *Cuddy alone and I.*[1]

In the nursery collection of *c.* 1783 the song begins :—

> There was a frog liv'd in a well, *Kitty alone, Kitty alone,*
> There was a frog liv'd in a well.
> There was a frog liv'd in a well, *Kitty alone and I.*
> And a farce mouse in a mill,
> *Cock me cary, Kitty alone, Kitty alone and I.*

(c. 1783, p. 4.)

The origin and meaning of this burden remains obscure.

The antiquity and the wide popularity of these verses are further shown by a song written in imitation of it, called *A Ditty on a High Amore at St. James,* and set to a popular tune, which dates from before 1714. It is in verse, and begins :—

[1] Sharpe, Ch. K., *Ballad Book,* 1824, p. 87.

Great Lord Frog and Lady Mouse, *Crackledom hee, crack-
    ledom ho,*
Dwelling near St. James' house, *Cocki mi chari chi;*
Rode to make his court one day,
In the merry month of May,
When the sun shone bright and gay, *twiddle come, tweedle
    dee.*[1]

In the accepted nursery version the song
begins :—

A frog he would a wooing ride, *heigho, says Rowley,*
Whether his mother would let him or no,
With a roly-poly, gammon and spinach,
Heigho, says Anthony Rowley.

This burden is said by a correspondent of
Notes and Queries to have been first inserted in
the old song as a burden by Liston. His song,
entitled *The Love-sick Frog*, with an original tune
by C. E. H., Esq. (perhaps Charles Edward Horn),
and an accompaniment by Thomas Cook, was
published by Goulding & Co., Soho Square, in
the early part of the nineteenth century (*N. &*
Q., I, 458). The burden has been traced back
to the *jeu d'esprit* of 1809 on the installation of
Lord Grenville as Chancellor of Oxford, which
another correspondent quotes from memory :—

[1] Chappell, loc. cit., p. 561.

Mister Chinnery then an M.A. of great parts,
Sang the praises of Chancellor Grenville.
Oh! He pleased all the ladies and tickled their
    hearts,
But then we all know he's a Master of Arts.
With a rowly, powly, gammon and spinach,
Heigh ho! says Rowley.   (*N. & Q.*, II, 27.)

Another variation of the song of *The Frog
and the Mouse* of about 1800 begins:—

There was a frog lived in a well, *heigho, crowdie!*
And a merry mouse in a mill, *with a howdie, crowdie*, etc.
                                    (*N. & Q.*, II, 110.)

This expression, *heigho, crowdie*, contains a call
to the crowd to strike up. The crowd is the
oldest kind of British fiddle, which had no neck
and only three strings. It is mentioned as a
British instrument already by the low Latin
poet Fortunatus towards the close of the sixth
century: "Chrotta Britannia canat." The instrument is well known to this day in Wales as the
crwth.

The word crowdy occurs also as a verb in one
of the numerous nursery rhymes referring to
scenes of revelry, at which folk-humour pictured
the cat making music:—

Come dance a jig to my granny's pig,
With a rowdy, rowdy, dowdy ;
Come dance a jig to my granny's pig,
And pussy cat shall crowdy.   (1846, p. 141.)

This verse and a number of others go back to the festivities that were connected with Twelfth Night. Some of them preserve expressions in the form of burdens which have no apparent sense ; in other rhymes the same expressions have the force of a definite meaning. Probably the verses in which the words retain a meaning have the greater claim to antiquity.

Thus among the black-letter ballads is a song[1] which is found also in the nursery collection of 1810 under the designation *The Lady's Song in Leap Year*.

Roses are red, *diddle diddle*, lavender's blue,
If you will have me, *diddle diddle*, I will have you.
Lillies are white, *diddle diddle*, rosemary's green,
When you are king, *diddle, diddle*, I will be queen.
Call up your men, *diddle, diddle*, set them to work,
Some to the plough, *diddle, diddle*, some to the cart.
Some to make hay, *diddle, diddle*, some to cut corn,
While you and I, *diddle, diddle*, keep the bed warm.

(1810, p. 46.)

[1] *Roxburgh Collection*, IV, 433.

D

Halliwell cites this song in a form in which the words are put into the lips of the king, and associates it with the amusements of Twelfth Night :—

Lavender blue, *fiddle faddle*, lavender green,
When I am king, *fiddle faddle*, you shall be queen, etc.

(1849, p. 237.)

The expression *diddle diddle* according to Murray's Dictionary means to make music without the utterance of words, while *fiddle faddle* is said to indicate nonsense, and to fiddle is to fuss. But both words seem to go back to the association of dancing, as is suggested by the songs on Twelfth Night, or by the following nursery rhyme which refers to the same celebration.

A cat came fiddling out of the barn,
With a pair of bagpipes under her arm,
She could sing nothing but fiddle cum fee,
The mouse has married the humble bee ;
Pipe, cat, dance, mouse ;
We'll have a wedding in our good house.

(1842, p. 102.)

The following variation of this verse occurs in the *Nursery Songs* published by Rusher :—

A cat came fiddling out of a barn,
With a pair of bagpipes under her arm,
She sang nothing but fiddle-de-dee,
Worried a mouse and a humble bee.
Puss began purring, mouse ran away,
And off the bee flew with a wild huzza!

In both cases the cat was fiddling, that is moving to instrumental music without the utterance of words, and called upon the others to do so while she played the pipes. Her association with an actual fiddle, however, is preserved in the following rhyme which I cite in two of its numerous variations :—

Sing hey diddle diddle, the cat and the fiddle,
The cow jump'd over the moon !
The little dog laughed to see such sport,
And the dish lick't up the spoon.

(1797, cited by Rimbault.)

Sing hey diddle diddle, the cat and the fiddle,
The cow jumped over the moon ;
The little dog laughed to see such craft,
And the dish ran away with the spoon.

(c. 1783, p. 27.)

This rhyme also refers to the revelry which accompanied a feast, probably the one of Twelfth Night also.

CHAPTER IV

RHYMES IN TOY-BOOKS

MANY of our longer nursery pieces first appeared in print in the diminutive toy-books already described, which represent so curious a development in the literature of the eighteenth century. These books were sometimes hawked about in one or more sheets, which were afterwards folded so as to form a booklet of sixteen, thirty-two, or sixty-four pages. Others were issued sewn and bound in brilliant covers, at a cost of as much as a shilling or eighteen pence. Usually each page contained one verse which was illustrated by an appropriate cut. In the toy-books which tell a consecutive story, the number of verses of the several pieces seem to have been curtailed or enlarged in order to fit the required size of the book.

It is in these toy-books that we first come

across famous nursery pieces such as the *Alphabet*
which begins :—

> A was an Archer, who shot at a frog,
> B was a blind man, and led by a dog . . . etc.

This first appeared in *A Little Book for Little
Children* by T. W., sold at the Ring in Little
Britain. It contains a portrait of Queen Anne,
and probably goes back to the early part of the
eighteenth century.

The Topbook of all, already mentioned, which
is of about 1760, contains the oldest version
that I have come across of the words used
in playing *The Gaping, Wide-mouthed, Waddling
Frog*, each verse of which is illustrated by
a rough cut. Again, *The Tragic Death of
A, Apple Pie*, which, as mentioned above, was
cited as far back as 1671, forms the contents of a
toy-book issued by J. Evans about the year 1791
at the price of a farthing. *The Death and Burial
of Cock Robin* fills a toy-book which was
published by J. Marshall, London, and again by
Rusher at Banbury ; both editions are undated.
Again *The Courtship, Marriage, and Picnic
Dinner of Cock Robin and Jenny Wren* form the

contents of a toy-book dated 1810 and published by Harris, and *The Life and Death of Jenny Wren* appeared in a toy-book dated 1813, issued by J. Evans.

Another famous toy-book contained *The Comic Adventures of Old Mother Hubbard and her Dog*. This story was first issued in toy-book form by J. Harris, "successor to E. Newbery at the corner of St. Paul's Churchyard," probably at the beginning of 1806, at the cost of eighteen pence. A copy of the second edition, which mentions the date 1 May, 1806, is at the British Museum. It contains the words "to T. B. Esquire, M.P. county of XX, at whose suggestion and at whose house these notable sketches were first designed, this volume is with all suitable deference dedicated by his humble servant S. C. M." The coffin which is represented in one of the cuts in the book bears the initials S. C. M., and the date 1804. This inscribing of the author's initials on a coffin is quite in keeping with the tone of toy-book literature.

In October, 1805, J. Harris had published *Whimsical Incidents, or the Power of Music, a poetic tale by a near relation of Old Mother Hub-bard,* which has little to recommend it, and contains nothing on the dog.   On its first page stands a verse which figures independently as a nursery rhyme in some later collections :—

> The cat was asleep by the side of the fire,
> Her mistress snor'd loud as a pig,
> When Jack took the fiddle by Jenny's desire,
> And struck up a bit of a jig.   (1810, p. 33.)

J. Harris also published in March, 1806, *Pug's Visit, or the Disasters of Mr. Punch,* a sequel to the *Comic Adventures of Mother Hubbard and her Dog.*   This has a dedication framed in the same style, "To P. A. Esquire . . . by his humble servant W. F."

The success of the *Comic Adventures of Mother Hubbard and her Dog* was instantaneous and lasting.   In *The Courtship of Jenny Wren,* which is dated 1810, while its cuts bear the date 1806, Parson Rook is represented carrying "Mother Hubbard's book," and a foot-note is added to the effect that "upwards of ten thousand copies of this celebrated work have been distributed in various parts of the country in a few months."

The *Comic Adventures* were read all over London and in the provinces, both in the original and in pirated editions, of which I have seen copies issued by J. Evans of Long Lane, West Smithfield ; by W. S. Johnson of 60 St. Martin's Lane ; by J. Marshall of Aldermary Churchyard; and by others. A very diminutive toy-book containing verses of the tale of Mother Hubbard, illustrated with rough cuts, is on view at South Kensington Museum among the exhibits of A. Pearson. I do not know its publisher.

The *Comic Adventures of Mother Hubbard* are usually told in fourteen verses, which refer to the dame's going to the cupboard, to her going for bread, for a coffin, for tripe, beer, wine, fruit, a coat, a hat, a wig, shoes, hose, and linen. The story ends :—

> The dame made a curtsey, the dog made a bow,
> The dame said, " Your servant," the dog said " Bow-
> wow."

But some editions have an additional rhyme on the dame's going for fish ; and the edition at South Kensington has the verse :—

Old Mother Hubbard sat down in a chair,
And danced her dog to a delicate air ;
She went to the garden to buy him a pippin,
When she came back the dog was skipping.

In the edition of Rusher, instead of "the dog made a bow," we read "Prin and Puss made a bow."

In Halliwell's estimation the tale of Mother Hubbard and her dog is of some antiquity, "were we merely to judge," he says, "of the rhyme of laughing to coffin in the third verse."

She went to the undertaker's to buy him a coffin,
When she came back the poor dog was laughing.

But it seems possible also that the author of the poem had running in his mind a verse containing this rhyme, which occurs already in the *Infant Institutes* of 1797, where it stands as follows :—

There was a little old woman and she liv'd in a shoe,
She had so many children, she didn't know what to do.
She crumm'd 'em some porridge without any bread
And she borrow'd a beetle, and she knock'd 'em all o'
    th' head.
Then out went the old woman to bespeak 'em a coffin
And when she came back she found 'em all a-loffing.

This piece contains curious mythological allusions, as we shall see later.

It may be added that the nursery collection of 1810 (p. 37) contains the first verse only of Mother Hubbard, which favours the view expressed by Halliwell, that the compiler of the famous book did not invent the subject nor the metre of his piece, but wrote additional verses to an older story.

The association of Mother Hubbard and the dog may be relatively new, but the name Mother Hubbard itself has some claim to antiquity. For a political satire by Edmund Spenser was called *Prosopopeia or Mother Hubberd's Tale.* It was a youthful effort of the poet, and was soon forgotten. In this piece " the good old woman was height Mother Hubberd who did far surpass the rest in honest mirth," and who related the fable of the fox and the ape. Also Thomas Middleton in 1604 published *Father Hubburd's Tale, or the Ant and the Nightingale,* in the introduction to which he addressed the reader as follows :—" Why I call these Father Hubburd's tales, is not to have them called in again as the Tale of Mother

Hubburd. The world would shew little judgment in that i' faith ; and I should say then *plena stultorum omnia;* for I entreat (*i.e.* treat) here neither of rugged (*i.e.* ragged) bears or apes, no, nor the lamentable downfall of the old wife's platters—I deal with no such metal . . . etc."

We do not know that Spenser's tale was "called in again," nor does it mention ragged bears and platters. Middleton must therefore be referring to a different production to which obstruction was offered by the public authorities. In any case the name of Mother Hubburd, or Hubbard, was familiar long before the publication of the story of the dame and her dog.

Father Hubberd, who is mentioned by Middleton, figures in nursery lore also. A rhyme is cited which mentions him in connection with the traditional cupboard :—

> What's in the cupboard? says Mr Hubbard ;
> A knuckle of veal, says Mr Beal ;
> Is that all? says Mr Ball ;
> And enough too, says Mr Glue ;
> And away they all flew.   (*N. & Q.*, 7, IV, 166.)

Were they figured as cats ?

The form of verse of this piece on Father Hubbard reproduces the chiming of bells. The same form of verse is used also in the following :—

"Fire ! Fire !" says the town-crier ;
"Where, where ?" says Goody Blair ;
"Down the town," said Goody Brown ;
"I'll go and see 't," said Goody Fleet,
"So will I," said Goody Fry.   (1890, p. 315.)

The old play of *Ralph Roister Doister*, written about the year 1550, ends with a "peele of bells rung by the parish clerk," which is in the same form of verse :—

First bell : When dyed he, when dyed he ?
Second bell : We have him ! We have him !
Third bell : Roister doister, Roister doister.
Fourth bell : He cometh, he cometh.
Great bell : Our owne, our owne.

CHAPTER V

RHYMES AND BALLADS

VARIOUS nursery pieces deal with material which forms the subject of romantic ballads also. Romantic ballads, like popular songs, are preserved in a number of variations, for they were sung again and again to suit the modified taste of succeeding ages. Many romantic ballads retain much that is pre-Christian in disposition and sentiment. The finest collection of romantic ballads during recent times was made by Child,[1] who included the fireside versions of ballads that have come down to us through nursery litera- ture. Child puts forward the opinion that where we are in possession of a romantic and a fireside version of the same ballad, the latter is a late and degraded survival. But this hardly seems prob-

[1] Child, F. G., *English and Scottish Popular Ballads* 1894.

45

able, considering that the nursery version of the tale is usually simpler in form, and often consists of dialogue only.

In the estimation of Gregory Smith, the oldest extant examples of romantic ballads "do not date further back than the second and third quarter of the fifteenth century" (that is between 1425 and 1475), "since the way in which the incidents in these are presented, reflects the taste of that age."[1] This applies to romantic ballads that are highly complex in form. The fireside version of the same story may have flowed from the same source. The question hangs together with that of the origin of the ballad, which may have arisen in connection with dancing and singing, but the subject needs investigation.

Among our famous early ballads is that of *The Elfin Knight*, the oldest printed copy of which is of 1670.

It begins as follows :—

> My plaid awa', my plaid awa',
> And o'er the hill and far awa',
> And far awa' to Norrowa,

[1] Smith, G., *The Transition Period*, 1897, p. 180, in Saintsbury, *Periods of European Literature.*

My plaid shall not be blown awa'.
The Elfin Knight sits on yon hill,
Ba, ba, ba, lilli ba,
He blaws his horn both loud and shrill,
The wind has blawn my plaid awa',
He blows it east, he blows it west,
He blows it where he liketh best.[1]

The ballad goes on to describe how problems
were bandied between the Elfin Knight and a
lady.   The one on whom an impossible task was
imposed stood acquitted if he devised a task of no
less difficulty, which must first be performed by
his opponent.   Such flytings go far back in
literature.   In this case the Elfin Knight staked
his plaid, that is his life, on receiving the favour
of the lady, and he propounded to her three
problems, viz. of making a sack without a seam,
of washing it in a well without water, and of
hanging it to dry on a tree that never blossomed.
In reply, she claimed that he should plough an
acre of land with a ram's horn, that he should
sow it with a peppercorn, and that he should
reap it with a sickle of leather.   The problems
perhaps had a recondite meaning, and the ballad-

[1] Child, loc. cit., I, 6 ff.

monger probably found them ready to hand. For Child cites a version of the ballad in which the same flyting took place between a woman and "the auld, auld man," who threatened to take her as his own, and who turned out to be Death. The idea of a wooer staking his life on winning a lady is less primitive than that of Death securing a victim.

The same tasks without their romantic setting are preserved in the form of a simple dialogue, in the nursery collections of *c.* 1783 and 1810. In this case also it is the question of a wooer.

Man speaks.

Can you make me a cambrick shirt,
Parsley, sage, rosemary, and thyme,
Without any seam or needlework?
And you shall be a true lover of mine.
Can you wash it in yonder well? Parsley, etc.,
Where never spring water or rain ever fell.
Can you dry it on yonder thorn,
Which never bore blossom since Adam was born?

Maiden speaks.

Now you have asked me questions three,
I hope you will answer as many for me.
Can you find me an acre of land,
Between the salt water and the sea sand?

Can you plow it with a ram's horn,
And sow it all over with peppercorn?
Can you reap it with a sickle of leather,
And bind it up with a peacock's feather?

When you have done and finished your work,
Then come to me for your cambrick shirt.

(*c.* 1783, p. 10.)

On the face of it, it hardly seems likely that this version is descended from the romantic ballad.

The tasks that are here imposed on the man are set also in the form of a boast in a nursery song, in which they have so entirely lost their meaning as to represent a string of impossibilities.

My father left me three acres of land,
Sing sing, sing sing,
My father left me three acres of land,
Sing holly, go whistle and sing.
I ploughed it with a ram's horn,
And sowed it with one pepper corn.
I harrowed it with a bramble bush,
And reaped it with a little pen knife.
I got the mice to carry it to the mill,
And thrashed it with a goose's quill.
I got the cat to carry it to the mill,
The miller swore he would have her paw,
And the cat she swore she would scratch his face.

(*N. & Q.,* VII. 8.)

E

Another nursery piece is recorded by Halliwell which, in simple form relates concerning *Billy
my son* the sequence of events which underlies
the famous romantic ballad of Lord Randal.[1]
The story is current also in Scotland relating
to *The Croodin Doo* (1870, p. 51); it was told
also some eighty years ago in Lincolnshire, of
King Henry my son (*N. & Q.*, 8, VI, 427). The
romantic ballad in five verses, as told of Lairde
Rowlande, relates how he came from the woods
weary with hunting and expecting death. He
had been at his true love's, where he ate of the
food which poisoned his warden and his dogs. In
the nursery version the tragedy is told in the
following simple form :—

> Where have you been to-day, Billy my son?
> Where have you been to-day, my only man?—
> I've been a wooing, mother ; make my bed soon,
> For I'm sick at heart, and fain would lie down.
>
> What have you ate to-day, Billy my son?
> What have you ate to-day, my only man?—
> I've eat eel pie, mother ; make my bed soon,
> For I am sick at heart, and shall die before noon.
>
> (1849, p. 259.)

[1] *Ibid.*, I, 157 : Lord Randal.

Other nursery pieces deal with Tommy Linn, the Tam Linn of romance, who is the hero of many famous romantic ballads. The name of Tam Linn goes some way back in history. For the *Tayl of young Tamlene*, according to Vedderburn's *Complaint of Scotland*, of 1549, was told among a company of shepherds, and the name appears also as that of a dance, *A Ballett of Thomalyn*, as far back as 1558.[1]

According to the romantic ballads, Tam Linn fell under the influence of the fairies through sleeping under an apple tree, and they threatened to take him back as their own on Hallowe'en, when they rode abroad once in seven years and had the right to claim their due. Tam Linn told the woman who loved him that she must hold him fast, whatever shape he assumed owing to the enchantment of the witches, and that she must cast him into water as soon as he assumed the shape of a *gled*. He would then be restored to human form.

Tam Linn of romance figures in nursery lore as Tommy Linn. His exploits were printed by

[1] *Ibid.*, I, 256 : Tamlene.

Halliwell in one of the numerous versions that are current in the north. In these pieces Tommy Linn has only this in common with Tam Linn of romance, that he too is ready with a suggestion whatever mishap befalls.

Tommy Linn is a Scotchman born,
His head is bald and his beard is shorn ;
He has a cap made of a hare skin,
An alderman is Tommy Linn.

Tommy Linn has no boots to put on,
But two calves' skins and the hair it was on.
They are open at the side and the water goes in,
Unwholesome boots, says Tommy Linn.

Tommy Linn had no bridle to put on,
But two mouse's tails that he put on.
Tommy Linn had no saddle to put on,
But two urchins' skins and them he put on.

Tommy Linn's daughter sat on the stair,
O dear father, gin I be not fair?
The stairs they broke and she fell in,
You're fair enough now, says Tommy Linn.

Tommy Linn had no watch to put on,
So he scooped out a turnip to make himself one ;
He caught a cricket and put it within,
It's my own ticker, says Tommy Linn.

Tommy Linn, his wife, and wife's mother,
They all fell into the fire together ;
Oh, said the topmost, I've got a hot skin,
It's hotter below, says Tommy Linn.

(1849, p. 271.)

Several short nursery rhymes are taken from this, or other versions of this poem.   Among the pieces printed by Chambers we read—

> Tam o' the Lin and his bairns,
> Fell i' the fire in others' arms !
> Oh, quo' the bunemost, I ha'e a hot skin ! !
> It's hotter below, quo' Tam o' the Lin ! ! !
>
> (1870, p. 33.)

Sir Walter Scott in *Redgauntlet* cites a catch on *Sir Thom o' Lyne*.

In some nursery collections the adventures of Tommy Lin, the Scotchman, are appropriated to Bryan O'Lin, the Irishman.

> Bryan O'Lin had no watch to put on,
> So he scooped out a turnip to make himself one :
> He caught a cricket and put it within,
> And called it a ticker, did Bryan O'Lin.

> Bryan O'Lin had no breeches to wear,
> So he got a sheepskin to make him a pair :
> With the skinny side out and the woolly side in,
> Oh ! how nice and warm, cried Bryan O'Lin.
>
> (1842, p. 212.)

Many nursery rhymes which dwell on cats are formed on the model of these verses.   A rhyme that comes from America is as follows :—

Kit and Kitterit and Kitterit's mother,
All went over the bridge together.
The bridge broke down, they all fell in,
"Good luck to you," says Tom Bolin.

A modern collection of rhymes (1873, p. 136) gives this as follows :—

The two grey cats and the grey kits' mother,
All went over the bridge together ;
The bridge broke down, they all fell in,
May the rats go with you, sings Tom Bowlin.

The association of cats with Tommy Linn reappears in the rhyme in which Tommy, who in the romantic ballad begged immersion for himself, practised immersion on a cat. Perhaps the cat was figured as a witch, who, being suspected, was cast into the water in order to prove her witch-craft.

Ding dong bell, poor pussy has fall'n i' th' well,
Who threw her in?   Little Tom O' Linne,
What a naughty boy was that
To drown poor pussy cat,
That never did any harm,
But catch'd a mouse i' th' barn.

(1797, cited by Rimbault.)

Other variations of this rhyme mention Johnny Green (c. 1783, p. 23) and Tommy Quin (Rusher),

which, considering the relative antiquity of
Tommy Linn, are obvious degradations of this
name.

The rhyme in some collections is quoted in an
enlarged form :—

Who put her in ?   Little Tommy Lin,
Who pulled her out ?   Little Tommy [*or* Dickey] Stout.

I have heard also :—

Who put her in ?   Little Tommy Thin.
Who pulled her out ?   Little Tommy Stout.

Stout is perhaps a traditional name.   For it
occurs in the nursery piece on the old woman who
went to sleep out of doors and forgot her identity.
I know no earlier version of this piece in English
than the one recorded by Rimbault which begins :

There was a little woman as I've heard tell,
Who went to market her eggs for to sell.

It further relates how she went to sleep out of
doors, how the man Stout "cut her petticoats
round about," and how on waking she did not
know herself, and decided to go home and find
out if her dog knew her (1864, p. 6).   But the
story is an old one, for we come across it in

Grimm's *Fairy Tales*, where it forms a sequel to
" Kluge Else," (No. 35).   In this the part of Stout
is taken by the woman's husband, who hung her
skirt about with bells, and it is further stated that
the woman fell asleep when she was cutting corn.
The same story in a more interesting form was
recovered in Norway.   Here we read that the
woman fell asleep while she was cutting hemp,
which explains why her mind failed her.   For
hemp newly cut has strongly narcotic properties.
It was probably the herb which the witches
smoked in their diminutive clay-pipes in pre-
Christian times.   Presumably on account of these
narcotic properties sowing and cutting of hemp
were associated all over Europe with peculiar
dances, such as *Enfille aiguille*, our *Thread-the-
Needle*.   Its connection with heathen rites of divination is suggested by the well-known rhyme :—

> Hemp-seed I set, hemp-seed I sow,
> The young man whom I love,
> Come after me and mow.   (1890, p. 414.)

In this form the rhyme is also cited in *Mother
Bunch's Closet newly broke open*, as a charm to
secure the vision of one's future husband.

CHAPTER VI

RHYMES AND COUNTRY DANCES

M ANY true nursery rhymes go back to traditional dancing and singing games which
are now relegated to the playground, but which
were danced by rustics within the memory of
man, and which are heirs to the choral dances of
our heathen forefathers. For dancing in its origin
was no idle and unmeaning pastime. Dances
were undertaken for serious purposes, such as
warding off evil and promoting agricultural
growth, conceptions which hang closely together.
These dances formed part of festivities that took
place at certain times of the year. They were
accompanied by expressive words, and by actions
which were suited to the words, and which gave
the dance a dramatic character. Our carol is
related to the *caraula* that was prohibited among
heathen customs by Bishop Eligius of Noyon

(d. 659), in the north of France in the seventh century, and has the same origin as the *Choreia* of the Greeks, the *reihe* or *reigen* of Germany, the *karol* of Brittany, and the *caraula* of eastern Switzerland. In course of time the religious significance of the choral dance was lost and its practice survived as a sport. At a later stage still, it became a pastime of children and a diversion of the ballroom.

Among the dances that can be traced back through several stages, is the one which in its latest survival is known as the *Cotillon*. This is mentioned in England as far back as the year 1766. Burns in *Tam o' Shanter* speaks of it as " brand new from France." The peculiar features of the Cotillon as it is danced nowadays, include free choice of partners, the women being at liberty in one figure to choose the men, the drawing into the dance of the assembled company, and the presence of a cushion which is put to a variety of uses. The Cotillon usually concludes the ball.

In an earlier form the Cotillon is represented by the dance which was known in the seventeenth

century as *Joan Saunderson or the Cushion Dance*.
The way of dancing *Joan Saunderson* is described
in *The Dauncing Master, a collection of dances
with tunes for young people*, published by
H. Playford.   Of this the first volume was
issued in 1650, which was enlarged in subsequent editions, when further volumes were added.
The Dauncing Master of Playford shows how
traditional country dances were appropriated to
the ballroom, for many of these dance tunes,
such as *Mulberry Bush*, and *Green Sleeves*, correspond with the names of traditional dancing and
singing games.

In *Joan Saunderson or the Cushion Dance* as
described by Playford,[1] a cushion and a drinking-
horn were brought in by two dancers to the sound
of a fiddle.   The cushion-bearer locked the door
and pocketed the key, and danced round the room
alone.   Then he exchanged words with the fiddler
as to the need of finding a maid and pressing her
into the dance.   The name Joan Saunderson
being proposed, the cushion-bearer placed the
cushion before the woman of his choice, and

[1] Playford, *The Dauncing Master*, 1686, p. 206.

knelt upon it. She did the same, and drank from the horn. They kissed and danced together. The same ceremony was then gone through by the girl, who, when the name John Saunderson was proposed, approached the man of her choice bearing the cushion, the first dancer accompanying her. The ceremony was repeated again and again, alternately by man and woman, and as each dancer chose a partner, the number of those following the cushion-bearer increased. Finally the whole assembled company were drawn into the ring.

A scene in *Joan Saunderson* is said to be represented in a Dutch engraving of the year 1624 (1876, p. 254). *Joan Saunderson* is still danced in different parts of the country under the same or some similar name. In Derbyshire it is known as the *Cushion Dance*, and those who are drawn into the ring are addressed as John Sanders and Jane Sanders. In the Lowlands the dance is known as *Babbity Bowster*, bowster standing for bolster; in the north it is the *Whishin Dance*, whishin standing for cushion (1894, I, pp. 9, 87). The Cushion Dance was the last dance that was danced at a wedding,[1] and at Northampton it came at the conclusion of the May-Day festival (1876, p. 253).

In the Cotillon of the ballroom, the ring finally breaks up and the company dances in couples; the Cushion Dance leads up to the withdrawal of the married pair, and concludes with a romp. A later edition of *The Dauncing Master* (1698, p. 7), perhaps with a view to forestalling this, adds a sequel to the dance, according to which the game, after it had been wound, was unwound, that is, each dancer in turn bade farewell to his partner, and after doing so left the room.

The points of likeness between the Cotillon and the Cushion Dance are such as to favour the belief that they are connected. The free choice of partners, the presence of the cushion, the drawing in of the whole assembled company, and the fact that the dance terminates the ball, are peculiar to them both. The Cushion Dance being the older sport, preserves the association with weddings and with the May-Day festival,

[1] Murray's Dictionary : *Cushion Dance.*

which at one time was the occasion for mating and marriage.

The associations with mating and marriage are preserved also in a traditional game that is still played throughout the greater part of England, which is generally known as *Sally Waters*. The verses recited in playing it render it probable that the Cushion Dance is a later development of the game known as *Sally Waters*.

In playing *Sally Waters* the players stand in a ring, a boy and a girl alternately choose a partner and seal the bond by joining hands, or by kneeling, or by a kiss. The verses recited in playing the game were first recorded by Halliwell (1849, p. 133). Forty-nine further variations, used in different parts of the kingdom in playing the game, have been printed by Mrs. Gomme, who classed this among marriage games, (1894, II, 461). In the book of Playford the Cushion Dance is called also *Joan Saunderson*, and those who are pressed into the dance are designated as Joan Saunderson and John Saunderson, or as Jane Sanders and John Sanders. In playing the game of *Sally Waters* similar names are used.

Thus the children in Penzance stand in a ring and sing the following verse :—

> Little Sally Sander sitting in the Sander,
> Weeping and crying for her young man.
>
> (1894, No. 26.)

In playing the game in Liverpool they begin :—

> Little Polly Sanders sits on the sand, etc.
>
> (*Ibid.*, No. 42.)

The verses used in Yorkshire begin :—

> Little Alice Sander sat upon a cinder, etc.
>
> (*Ibid.*, No. 31.)

These names Sally Sander, Polly Sanders, etc., must be derived from the same source as Saunderson and Sanders of the Cushion Dance. A host of other rhymes current in the nursery deal with the same theme, and are formed on the same model. There is one step only from *little Sally Sander* of Penzance, *little Polly Sanders* of Liverpool, and *little Alice Sander who sat upon a cinder*, to the following rhymes which are included in different nursery collections. All these rhymes describe a person sitting and waiting, and most of them dwell on the idea of a seat or a cushion,

while the allusion to matters matrimonial, being
unsuitable to children, is altogether dropped.

> Little Polly Flinders sat among the cinders,
> Warming her pretty toes;
> Her mother came and caught her, and scolded her
>   little daughter,
> For spoiling her nice new clothes.   (1846, p. 212.)

> Little Miss Muffet sat on a tuffet,
> Eating of curds and whey,
> There came a great spider and sat down beside her
> And frightened Miss Muffet away. [1]

> Little Mary Ester sat upon a tester
> Eating of curds and whey ;
> There came a little spider and sat down beside her,
> And frightened Mary Ester away.   (1842, p. 61.)

Tuffet and tester are words for a footstool.

> Little Miss Mopsey sat in the shopsey,
> Eating of curds and whey ;
> There came a great spider who sat down beside her
> And frightened Miss Mopsey away.   (1842, p. 37.)

> Little Tom Tacket sits upon his cracket,
> Half a yard of cloth will make him a jacket,
> Make him a jacket and breeches to the knee,
> And if you will not have him, you may let him be.
>   (1842, p. 199.)

[1] *Songs for the Nursery*, published by Darton & Co.,
1812. The verses included in this collection were altered
with a view to rendering them more suitable for children.

Little Tom Tucker sings for his supper,
What shall he eat, but white bread and butter ;
How will he cut it, without e're a knife
And how will he be married without e're a wife.

(1744, p. 10 ; c. 1783, p. 56.)

Little Jack Horner sat in the corner,
Eating a [of] Christmas pie ;
He put in his thumb, and he took [pulled] out a plum,
And said [cried] " What a good boy am I ! "

Chorus: And what a good boy am I !   (c. 1783, p. 55.)

These verses as they here stand arranged, show an increasing deviation from the words used in playing the game of Sally Waters.

Tom Tucker and Jack Horner are names that go some way back in history.   For Brand states that at the revels kept at St. John's College, 1 November, 1607, a Christmas Lord of the Revels was chosen as Thomas Tucker.[1]   A dance tune of the *Dauncing Master* was called *Tom Tucker* also.[2]

The name of Jacky Horner was familiar to Carey about the year 1720, as mentioned above. *Little Jack Horner* was a well-known tune, and there is a direction in the Grub Street opera that

[1] Brand, *Popular Antiquities*, I, 219.
[2] *The Dauncing Master*, 1686, p. 130.

F

the chorus shall be sung to this melody.[1]   A chapbook of the latter half of the eighteenth century bears the title, *The Pleasant History of Jack Horner, containing his Witty Tricks*, etc. It cites the familiar rhyme, and further describes the pranks that the hero played upon women. This association and the name recall the expressions *hornified*, that is a cuckold;[2] *horning*, a mock serenade "without which no wedding would be complete"; and *Horn Fair*, a time of unusual licence, kept up in Kent: "all was fair at Horn Fair" (1876, p. 387).

[1] Whitmore, loc. cit., p. 27.
[2] Murray's Dictionary: *Horning*.

CHAPTER VII

THE GAME OF *SALLY WATERS*

THE game of *Sally Waters* calls for further comment. In this game, as already mentioned, the players stand in a circle, boy and girl alternately choose a partner, while the friends stand around and chant the verses. In these lies the interest of the game. For these words in the fifty variations collected by Mrs. Gomme, all give expression to the same sequence of ideas. There is the call to Sally to go through the ceremony of sprinkling the pan or watering the can. This is followed by a chorus that urges that a choice be made. When this is made and sealed by joining hands, or by kneeling, or by a kiss, the chorus utters wishes for a prosperous union. Similar traits appear in the games known as *Pretty Little Girl of Mine*, *The Lady of the Mountain*, and *Kiss in the Ring*, which, in a less pronounced form, give expression to the same ideas.

The verses used in playing *Sally Waters* in Dorsetshire are among the most meaningful, and stand as follows :—

Sally, Sally Waters, sprinkle in the pan,
Rise, Sally ; rise, Sally, and choose a young man ;
Choose [*or* bow] to the east, choose [*or* bow] to the west
[*Or* choose for the best one, choose for the worst one],
Choose the pretty girl [*or* young man] that you love best.

And now you're married, I wish you joy,
First a girl and then a boy ;
Seven years after son and daughter,
And now young people, jump over the water.

(1894, Nr. 1.)

These verses and the fact that *Sally Waters* is related to the Cushion Dance that is danced at weddings, render it probable that *Sally Waters* originated in a marriage celebration of heathen times. The formula in the Dorsetshire version of the game concludes with a direction to the young couple to "jump over the water." In the Somersetshire version the direction is "kiss each other and come out of the water" (1894, No. 3); in the Shropshire variation, "kiss and shake hands and come out" (1894, No. 14); in the London variation, "kiss before you go out of the water." (Appendix.)

Dipping was an accepted ceremonial during heathen times, which recovered or revealed a person's true identity as in the case of Tam Linn, or of the suspected witch who was thrown into the water. Dipping constituted part of definite celebrations. For the ceremonial of "dipping" formed part of the May-Day festival as it was kept in Northampton, while in Cornwall the saying is current: "The first of May is dipping day" (1876, p. 235). May-Day was a great day for contracting matrimonial alliances in the heathen past, and is at present avoided because of its riotous associations.

Judging from the verses used in playing Sally Waters, the union between the parties was contracted conditionally for seven years only. Seven years are definitely mentioned in sixteen out of fifty variations of the game. The same period is mentioned also in fourteen out of the twenty-five variations of the verses used in playing *Pretty Little Girl of Mine*, and in three out of seven variations of the verses used in playing *The Lady on the Mountain*.

Mrs. Gomme, in discussing the game of Sally

Waters, cites various expressions which show that the marriage vow is still popularly looked upon as binding for a certain period only, sometimes for seven years (1894, II, 177). I find this corroborated by remarks I have gleaned from country-folk. Thus a woman whose husband had gone from her, after seven years felt justified in looking upon him as dead, and had the bell tolled for his funeral.

Time-reckoning by seven years goes far back in history, and is still the rule in many legal arrangements. Seven years of plenty succeeded seven years of famine in Egypt. Once in seven years the fairies rode out to claim their due. Some festivities happened only once in seven years. The curious custom of *bumping*, that is, of two persons taking up by the arms any persons whom they met, and swinging them to and fro, was observed on Ganging Day (29 September) once in seven years at Bishop's Stortford (1876, p. 380). At Bradford also a septennial festival was kept in honour of Jason and the Golden Fleece and St. Blaize on 3 February (1876, p. 60). Similarly a dance known as the Metzger-

sprung was danced at Munich once in seven years
to keep off the plague (Bo., p. 44).

The mention of seven years in the marriage
game may indicate that the marriage was broken
off after seven years if the stipulated conditions
failed to be fulfilled. These conditions were that
the children born of the union should include one
of either sex. Mrs. Gomme, in connection with
this stipulation, remarks that a marriage is still
popularly reckoned incomplete from which there
is not male and female offspring. She also points
out that the expression "choose for the best,
choose for the worst" of the marriage game, is
related to the words "for better, for worse" of
the vernacular portion of the English marriage
service. The expressions "worst and best," or
"wisest and best," occur in thirteen out of the
fifty versions of words; instead of these, "choose
east and choose west" occur in twenty-two out of
the fifty versions (1894, II, 168). It is difficult
to decide which is the more primitive form of the
verse; I fancy the latter.

The ceremony of choosing was led up to by
sprinkling the pan, which is mentioned in twenty-

one out of fifty variations of the game; *watering the can* stands in twelve others. The pan was specially associated with women as housekeepers, and, together with the cradle, is mentioned as one of the first essentials in setting up house in the game of *Wallflowers*.[1]

Judging from the game of *Sally Waters* as played in Bucks, a " mother" actually presided at the game, who directed her daughters to sprinkle the pan, and their being included among those from whom a choice was made, depended on their successfully doing so. To the words of the game as played in Bucks, I have added in brackets an indication how the words were probably distributed :—

(Half chorus) : Sally, Sally Walker, sprinkled in the pan.
(Other half) :   What did she sprinkle for?
(Answer) :   For a young man.
(Mother) :   Sprinkle, sprinkle daughter, and you shall
                 have a cow.

---

[1] Gomme, loc. cit.: *Wallflowers* :—
Mister Moffit is a very good man,
He came to the door with a hat ın his hand,
He pulled up his cloak and showed me the ring ;
To-morrow, to-morrow the wedding begins.
First he bought a frying pan, then he bought the cradle,
And then one day the baby was born.   Rock, rock the
    cradle.   (No. 32.)

(Daughter):   I cannot sprinkle, mother, because I don't
                 know how.

(Mother):   Sprinkle, daughter, sprinkle, and you
                 shall have a man.

(Daughter):   I cannot sprinkle, mother, but I'll do
                 the best I can.

(Chorus):   Pick and choose, but don't you pick me,
                 Pick the fairest you can see.

(Man):   The fairest that I can see is . . . Come to
                 me! (1894, No. 23.)

This is followed by the usual marriage formula.

A similar dialogue is included amongst the Nursery Rhymes of Halliwell, in which the daughter is directed to whistle, a word which formerly conveyed the idea of uttering imprecations in a low voice, and which was condemned in a woman since it marked her out for a witch. The verse stands as follows :—

Whistle daughter, whistle, whistle for a cradle.
I cannot whistle, mammy, 'deed I am not able.

Whistle daughter, whistle, whistle for a cow,
I cannot whistle, mammy, 'deed I know not how.

Whistle, daughter, whistle, whistle for a man,
I cannot whistle, mammy; whew! Yes, I believe I can.
                     (1846, p. 219.)[1]

---

[1] Cf. A whistling woman and a crowing hen
      Are neither fit for God or man. (1892, p. 506.)
Also: Une femme qui siffle et une poule qui crie
          Porte malheur dans la maison.

If the words used in playing *Sally Waters* are analysed, it will be seen that the name Sally occurs in forty-four out of fifty variations, and that in twenty-four variations the name is associated with water. It is combined with water especially in the south and the south-west of England. Away from this district we have the name Sally Walker, in Shropshire, Bucks, Yorkshire, Scotland, and Ireland ; the name Sally Salter in Yorkshire and Lincoln ; the names Sally Sander in Penzance, Polly Sanders in Liverpool, and so forth. Obviously, Sally Waters is the oldest form of the name. This view is accepted by Mrs. Gomme, who was, however, at a loss to account for the wide use of the name Sally Waters. But, in classing the variations of words of the game according to the reasonableness of their contents, she placed foremost as most meaningful the verses that hailed from Dorsetshire, Somerset, and Devonshire, where the form Sally Waters is in use. It is to this district, therefore, that we must turn for the origin of the game of *Sally Waters.*

On turning to the history of the British past in these districts, we find that the Romans when they came to Bath found this spot far famed for its waters. The name by which they knew the place was *Aquæ Solis*, but the word *Solis* did not stand for the sun as a male divinity, but for *Sul*, the presiding female divinity of the place. For the Roman temple built at Bath was dedicated to the goddess Sulis-Minerva, and the name Sul, both with and without the name of Minerva, occurs among the noted inscriptions.[1] It was a common practice with the Romans to couple the name of one of their own divinities with that of a local divinity, and Minerva, in her capacity of a healing goddess, was here associated with Sul, the female divinity of the waters. On the façade of the temple a medallion is represented. Inside it is the head of a goddess with her hair tied together over her forehead, and a crescent moon is behind her. The moon is an emblem which is not associated with Minerva elsewhere, and the head on the medallion must therefore represent Sul. Sul was the presiding divinity at Bath, and an altar was also discovered which was dedicated to the Sulevæ.

[1] Scarth, H. M., *Aquæ Solis, Notices on Roman Bath*, 1864, pp. 16 ff., 22 ff., etc.

A similar altar has been discovered at Nismes, which is dedicated to *Suliviæ Idennicæ Minervæ*. Scarth, in his history of Roman Bath, cites Mr. Roach Smith on these Sulevæ, who "appear to have been sylphs, the tutelary divinities of rivers, fountains, hills, roads, villages and other localities against whom were especially directed in the fifth and subsequent centuries the anathemas of Christian councils, missionaries, and princes."[1] Taking this evidence into consideration, is it far-fetched to suggest that Sally Waters of the traditional marriage game, which, in its most meaningful form, is still played in the districts surrounding Bath, may be related to Sul of the waters of Bath, and to her followers, or ministrants, the Sulevæ?

We know nothing further of Sul as far as our islands are concerned. But in Central France a female impersonation of the sun is still called upon as *La Soule*, and St. Solange, patron saint of Berry, who is represented with a light over her forehead, is looked upon as heir to her in the pantheon of Christian saints. Sulis also was a place-name in Brittany during Roman times,

[1] *Ibid.*, p. 53.

situated somewhere between Auray and Quimper. It seems probable that the site is identical with that of the present St. Anne d'Auray, famous for its holy waters, which are still sought in pilgrimage from far and near. The enormous stone basin into which pilgrims are dipped, remains its most curious feature.

In Scandinavian nursery lore we also come across a *Fru Sole*, the mother of many daughters, who sat in heaven, and across *Fru Soletopp*, who distributed gifts. These names may be related to Sul of the waters of Bath, or to Sally of our game, or to both. However this may be, the wide distribution of the game known as *Sally Waters*, and its peculiar connection with the south-west of England, induce the belief that there is some relation between Sally of the game, and Sul, the divinity of the waters.

CHAPTER VIII

THE LADY OF THE LAND

ASSOCIATIONS dating from heathen times are preserved in other traditional games, the full meaning of which becomes apparent only when we compare these with their foreign parallels. Some of these games in their cruder and more primitive forms are sports, in which dialogue takes the place of rhymed verses, and in which the characters that are introduced are frequently spoken of as animals.

Among the dancing and singing games first described by Halliwell is one called by him *The Lady of the Land.* In this game one side is taken by a mother and her daughters, the other by a second woman, and the game consists in the daughters changing sides. The verses that are recited are as follows:—

78

Here comes a woman from Babyland,
With three small children in her hand.
One can brew, the other can bake,
The other can make a pretty round cake.
One can sit in the garden and spin,
Another can make a fine bed for a king.
Pray m'am will you take one in?

(1846, p. 121.)

One child is then pointed out and passes to the other side, and this is continued till all are selected.

Twelve further variations of the words used in playing this game were recovered from different parts of the country by Mrs. Gomme (1894, I, 313). Of these two, one from Shropshire (No. 3) and one from the Isle of Wight (No. 6), like that of Halliwell, designate the woman as "from Babyland." Others, from the Isle of Man and from Galloway (Appendix), describe her as from Babylon, while further variations mention Sandiland (No. 9), Cumberland (Berks, No. 8), and others. The word Babyland, which occurs in three out of thirteen variations of the game, is probably the original one, for it has a parallel in the corresponding German game in the name *Engelland,* the land of the spirits of the unborn.

The Babyland game in a more primitive form is known as *Little Dog I call you,* in which the players also change sides (1894, I, 330). In this game, the one side is taken by a girl who looks after a number of children, the other by a girl who is designated as *Little Dog,* and who stands apart. The children secretly impart their wishes to their owner or leader, who warns them against laughing, and then calls the Little Dog and tells him to pick out the child who has expressed such and such a wish. Should this child laugh by inadvertence, she at once goes over to the Little Dog. If not, the dog is left to guess who has imparted the wish, and by doing so he secures the child. If he fails to guess aright, the child goes and stands behind the leader and is altogether removed out of the reach of the Little Dog. This is continued till all belong to one side or the other, and the game concludes with a tug of war.

The games of *The Lady of the Land* and *Little Dog* have parallels in the foreign game of

children changing sides, fourteen variations of
which were collected from different parts of
northern Europe by Mannhardt (M., p. 273).
The closest parallel to *The Lady of the Land* is
played in Belgium, in which sides are taken by
two leaders, of whom the one has many daughters
and the other has none. The game is called
Riche et pauvre and the following verses are
sung :—

> Je suis pauvre, je suis pauvre, Anne Marie Jacqueline ;
> Je suis pauvre dans ce jeu d'ici.—
> Je suis riche, je suis riche, Anne Marie Jacqueline ;
> Je suis riche dans ce jeu d'ici.—
> Donnez-moi un de vos enfants, Anne Marie Jacqueline,
> Donnez-moi un de vos enfants, dans ce jeu d'ici.
>
> (M., No. 13.)

"I am poor, I am poor in this game, I am rich in this
game. Give me one of your children, in this game."

This is continued as in the Babyland game
till every child has had its turn. There is no
sequel.

In the German game the woman who owns the
children is called sometimes Mary, sometimes
Witch, but usually she has the name of a heathen
divinity. Thus in Mecklenburg she is *Fru Goden*

G

or *Fru Gol* (No. 11). Gode is the name of a mother divinity, who, as *Godmor*, is the mother of Thor (Gr., p. 209, note). In the game as played in Prussia (No. 10), in Elsass (No. 3), in Swabia (No. 2), and in Aargau (No. 4), she is *Frau Ros* or *Frau Rose*, that is Lady Ros or Rose; while in Pommerellen she is either *Ole Moder Rose* or *Ole Moder Taersche* (No. 1), a word that signifies witch. In Holstein, on the other hand, the alternative is recorded as *Fru Rosen* or *Mutter Marie*, Mother Mary (No. 9), while in Appenzell (No. 5) and near Dunkirk (No. 6) the owner of the children is *Marei Muetter Gotts*, i.e. Mary the Mother of God. Mannhardt points out that Ross, sometimes Rose, is the name of a German mother divinity who occurs frequently in German folk-lore. I have come across Mother Ross in our own chapbook literature, where the name may be traditional also. Mary indicates the substitution of a Christian name in the place of the older heathen one. In Sweden the owner of many babes is *Fru Sole*, who is represented as sitting in heaven surrounded by her daughters, who are described as chickens (No. 14).

The game of securing children is called in Switzerland *Das Englein aufziehen* (No. 5), that is, "the drawing forth of an angel." The word *Engel*, angel, according to the information collected by Mannhardt, originally designates the spirit that awaits re-birth. For the heathen inhabitants of Northern Europe, including the Kelts, were unable to realize individual death. They held that the living spirit passed away with death, but continued in existence, and again reappeared under another shape. In the civilization that belonged to the mother age, these spirits or angels that awaited re-birth, peopled the realm which was associated with divine mothers or mother divinities. At a later period, transferred into Christian belief, they were pictured as a host of winged babes, whom we find represented in mediaeval art hovering around the Virgin Mother and Child.

The land in which the unborn spirits dwelt, is generally spoken of in German nursery and folk rhymes as *Engelland*, an expression which forms a direct parallel to the expression Babyland of our game. Thus the *Woman of Babyland*, like

Frau Rose or *Frau Gode* of the German game, was in all probability a divine mother, who was the owner of the spirits or babes that awaited re-birth.

In the estimation of Mannhardt, the game in which children are drawn from one woman into the possession of the other, preserves the relics of a ceremonial connected with the cult of the mother divinity. It visibly set forth how the spirits of the departed were drawn back into life (M., p. 319). Perhaps we may go a step further. The study of folk-lore has taught us that to simulate a desired result is one way of working for its attainment. Women who were desirous of becoming mothers, both in England and in Germany, were wont to rock an empty cradle. They also visited particular shrines. Of the rites which they practised there we know nothing. Perhaps the Babyland game originated not as an ideal conception, but preserves the relics of a rite by which women sought to promote mother-hood. This assumption is supported by various features that are incidental to the game.

Thus the game, both in England and abroad,

is essentially a girls' game, and the words that are used indicate that it is played by them only. Even where the generality of the players are designated as " children," the leaders are invariably girls.

Again, in some versions of the foreign game (Nos. 8, 9) there is mention of salt. The woman who asks for a child, complains that she has lost those that were given to her; she is told that she ought to have sprinkled them with salt (No. 8). Sprinkling with salt is still observed at Christian baptism in some districts, and such sprinkling is said to make a child safe.[1]

Again, in the game as played abroad the child that is chosen is put to the test if it can be made to laugh (Nos. 2, 4, 5, 8). In the game of *Little Dog* also, the child that laughs passes into the keeping of a new owner. Laughing indicates quickening into life, and in folk-lore generally the child that refrains from laughing is reckoned uncanny. Numerous stories are told of the changeling that was made to laugh and dis-

---

[1] Cf. Addy, S. O., *House Tales and Traditional Remains*, 1895, pp. 86, 120.

appeared, when the real child was found restored to its cradle.

Again, in the foreign game the player who seeks to secure a child speaks of herself as lame, and limps in order to prove herself so (Nos. 1, 2, 14). In one instance she attributes her limping to a bone in her leg. Limping, in the estimation of Mannhardt, is peculiar to the woman who has borne children (M., p. 305). For in German popular parlance the woman who is confined, is said to have been bitten by the stork who brought the child.

A reminiscence of this idea lurks in our proverb rhyme :—

> The wife who expects to have a good name,
> Is always at home as if she were lame ;
> And the maid that is honest, her chiefest delight
> Is still to be doing from morning till night.[1]

Again, in one version of the foreign game the children that are won over are given the names of dogs, and when their former owner attempts to get them back, they rush at her and bark (No. 1). This corresponds to our game of *Little Dog*, in

[1] Bohn, H., *A Handbook of Proverbs*, 1901, p. 43.

which the child that stands apart is addressed as
"Little Dog I call you." Grimm declared himself at a loss to account for the fact that a dog
was associated with the Norns or Fate-maidens
who assisted at childbirth (Gr., p. 339); Mannhardt cites the belief that the spirits of the dead
were sometimes spoken of as dogs (M., p. 301);
and in England there also exists a superstition
that the winds that rush past at night are dogs,
the so-called Gabriel hounds or ratchets (cf.
below, p. 165).

Features preserved in other games contain
similar suggestions which are worth noting.

Thus in the game known as *Drop-handkerchief*
one girl holding a kerchief goes round the others
who are arranged in a circle, saying :—

> I have a little dog and it won't bite you
> It won't bite you, it won't bite you [*ad lib.*]
> It *will* bite you.   (1894, I, 109.)

The person on whom *the little dog* is bestowed is
" bitten "; that is, she is in the same predicament
as the German woman who is bitten by the stork,
and the limping woman of the German Babyland
game.

In playing *Drop-handkerchief* in Deptford the children sing :—

> I had a little dog whose name was Buff,
> I sent him up the street for a pennyworth of snuff.
> He broke my box and spilt my snuff
> I think my story is long enough—
> 'Taint you, 'taint you, and 'taint you, but 'tis you.

(1894, I, p. 111.)

In the collection of Nursery Songs by Rusher stands the following rhyme :—

> I had a little dog and they called him Buff,
> I sent him to a shop to buy me snuff,
> But he lost the bag and spilt the stuff;
> I sent him no more but gave him a cuff,
> For coming from the mart without any snuff.

"Bufe" as a word for a dog occurs as far back as 1567.[1]

[1] Murray's Dictionary : *Bufe.*

CHAPTER IX

CUSTOM RHYMES

THE comparison of our short nursery rhymes with those current in other countries, next engages our attention. Halliwell has remarked that some of our rhymes are chanted by the children of Germany and Scandinavia, which to him strikingly exhibited the great antiquity and remote origin of these rhymes. The observation which he made with regard to the countries of Northern Europe, applies to the countries of Central and Southern Europe also. Scholarly collections of rhymes have been published during recent years in Scandinavia, Germany, France, Italy, Spain, and referring to special parts of these countries, which give us a fair insight into their nursery lore. (Cf., p. 212). The comparison of these collections with ours yields surprising results. Often the same thought is expressed in the same form of

89

verse. Frequently the same proper name reappears in the same connection. In many cases rhymes, that seem senseless taken by themselves, acquire a definite meaning when taken in conjunction with their foreign parallels. Judging from what we know of nursery rhymes and their appearance in print, the thought of a direct translation of rhymes in the bulk cannot be entertained. We are therefore left to infer, either that rhymes were carried from one country to another at a time when they were still meaningful, or else that they originated in different countries as the outcome of the same stratum of thought.

The sorting of nursery rhymes according to the number of their foreign parallels, yields an additional criterion as to the relative antiquity of certain rhymes. For those rhymes that embody the more primitive conceptions are those that are spread over the wider geographical area. The above inquiry has shown that pieces such as *Mother Hubbard* and *Three Blind Mice* are relatively new, and that all the rhymes formed on the model of *Little Miss Muffet* go back to the *Cushion Dance* and to the game of *Sally Waters*.

Rhymes of this kind are entirely without foreign parallels. On the other hand, calls, such as those addressed to the ladybird and the snail, and riddle-rhymes, such as that on *Humpty Dumpty*, have numerous and close parallels half across Europe.

The ladybird is the representative among ourselves of a large class of insects which were associated with the movement of the sun from the earliest times. The association goes back to the *kheper* or chafer of ancient Egypt, which has the habit of rolling along the ball that contains its eggs. This ball was identified as the orb of the sun, and the *kheper* was esteemed as the beneficent power that helped to keep it moving.

A like importance attached to the chafers that had the power of flying, especially to the ladybird (*Coccinella septem punctata*). In India the insect was called *Indragopas*, that is "protected by Indra." The story is told how this insect flew too near the sun, singed its wings, and fell back to the earth.[1]

In Greece the same idea was embodied in the

[1] De Gubernatis, *Zoological Mythology*, 1872, II, p. 209.

myth of Ikaros, the son of Dædalus, who flew too
near the sun with the wings he had made for himself, and, falling into the sea, was drowned.
Already the ancient Greeks were puzzled by this
myth, which found its reasonable explanation
in describing Ikaros as the inventor of sails.
He was the first to attach sails to a boat, and
sailing westwards, he was borne out to sea and
perished.

Among ourselves the ladybird is always
addressed in connection with its power of flight.
It is mostly told to return to its house or home,
which is in danger of being destroyed by fire, and
warned of the ruin threatening its children if
it fails to fly. But some rhymes address it on
matters of divination, and one urges it to bring
down blessings from heaven.

The rhyme addressed to the ladybird first
appears in the nursery collection of 1744, where
it stands as follows :—

> 1. Ladybird, ladybird, fly away home,
>   Your house is on fire, your children will burn.

Many variations of the rhyme are current in

different parts of the country, which may be tabulated as follows :—

2. Lady cow, lady cow, fly away home,
   Your house is on fire, your children all roam.
   (1892, p. 326.)

3. Ladycow, Ladycow, fly and be gone,
   Your house is on fire, and your children at home.
   (Hallamshire, 1892, p. 326.)

4. Gowdenbug, gowdenbug, fly away home,
   Yahr house is bahnt dun, and your children all gone.
   (Suffolk, *N. & Q.*, IV., 55.)

5. Ladybird, ladybird, eigh thy way home,
   Thy house is on fire, thy children all roam,
   Except little Nan, who sits in her pan
   Weaving gold laces as fast as she can.
   (Lancashire, 1892, p. 326.)

6. Ladybird, ladybird, fly away home,
   Your house is on fire, your children at home.
   They're all burnt but one, and that's little Ann,
   And she has crept under the warming pan.
   (Rusher's Series.)

7. Ladycow, ladycow, fly thy way home,
   Thy house is on fire, thy children all gone ;
   All but one, that ligs under a stone,
   Ply thee home, ladycow, ere it be gone.
   (1842, p. 204.)

8. Ladycow, Ladycow, fly away home,
   Thy house is on fire, thy children all gone ;
   All but one, and he is Tum,
   And he lies under the grindelstone.
   (Shropshire, 1892, p. 327.)

9. Dowdy cow, dowdy cow, ride away hame,
   Thy house is burnt, and thy bairns are ta'en ;
   And if thou means to save thy bairns,
   Take thy wings and fly away.
                    (N. Riding, Yorks., 1892, p. 327.)

10. Lady, lady landers, fly away to Flanders.
                    (Chambers, 1842, p. 43.)

11. Fly, ladybird, fly !
    North, south, east, or west,
    Fly to the pretty girl that I love best.
                    (1849, p. 5.)

12. King, king Golloway, up your wings and fly away,
    Over land and over sea ; tell me where my love
        can be.   (Kincardineshire, 1870, p. 201.)

13. Ladycow, ladycow, fly from my hand,
    Tell me where my true love stands,
    Up hill and down hill and by the sea-sand.
                    (1892, p. 119.)

14. Bishop, Bishop, Barnabee, tell me when my wedding
        will be.
    If it be to-morrow day,
    Ope your wings and fly away.
                    (Sussex, 1892, p. 119.)

15. Bishop, bishop, barnabee, tell me when my wedding
        will be.
    Fly to the east, fly to the west,
    Fly to them that I love best.
                    (*N. & Q.*, I., p. 132.)

16. Burnie bee, burnie bee, say when will your wedding be.
    If it be to-morrow day,
    Take your wings and fly away.
                    (Norfolk, 1849, p. 3.)

17. Bless you, bless you, bonnie bee, say when will your
    wedding be.
    If it be to-morrow day,
    Take your wings and fly away.
                              (M., p. 253, foot-note.)

18. God A'mighty's colly cow, fly up to heaven ;
    Carry up ten pound, and bring down eleven.
                              (Hampshire, 1892, p. 327.)

19. This ladyfly I take from the grass,
    Whose spotted back might scarlet red surpass.
    Fly ladybird, north, south, or east or west,
    Fly where the man is found that I love best.
                              (M., p. 417, citing Brand.)

The comparison of these rhymes with their
foreign parallels, of which a number were collected
by Mannhardt, shows that a rhyme current in
Saxony is very close to ours :—

> Himmelsküchlein, flieg aus !
> Dein Haus brennt,
> Deine kinder weinen alle miteinander.
>   (M., p. 349.)

"Heaven's little chicken, fly away ; thy house is on
fire, thy children are all crying."

Mannhardt was of opinion that the ladybird
rhyme originated as a charm intended to speed
the sun across the dangers of sunset, that is,
the "house on fire" or welkin of the West,

which is set aglow at sundown. Throughout the East a prayer is still uttered to the setting sun in order to ensure its safe return on the morrow.

The ladybird is known by a variety of names both in England and abroad. Among ourselves it is identified as a cow, a bird, or a bee, while the *lady* of our rhymes reappears as Mary in the German expression *Marienkäfer*. In Sweden the ladybird is addressed as *Jungfru Marias Nyckel-piga*, "the Lady Mary's keybearer," and this expression is explained by the story that the Virgin lost the keys of heaven, and that all the animals helped her to look for them. They were found by the ladybird, to whose care they are now entrusted. The keys of heaven have been interpreted as the lightning which opened the floodgates of heaven. For the mother divinities were credited with making the weather, with giving rain, and with washing. This latter association lingers in the Scottish ladybird rhyme, in which the ladybird is addressed as landers, i.e. laundress (M., p. 250, foot-note).

In Potsdam they sing :—

Marienwörmken flīg furt,
Flīg furt nach Engelland !
Engelland ist zugeschlossen,
Schlüssel davon abgebrochen.

(M., p. 347.)

"Insect of Mary, fly away, fly away to Engelland. Engelland is locked, its key is broken."

The rhyme thus combines the idea of the keys of heaven with *Engelland*, the home of the unborn spirits, and with Mary, to whom the insect is dedicated.

Many of our ladybird rhymes refer to the danger that is threatening, probably from sunset or the direction of the West, but one person is safe. It is little Nan, who sits weaving gold laces. Spinning gold or silk was a prerogative of the mother divinities who sat in heaven (Gr., 223, M., 705). Another rhyme calls her Ann. Nan or Ann reappears in the corresponding ladybird rhymes of Switzerland and Swabia. In Aargau they sing :—

Goldchäber, flüg uf, uf dine hoche Tanne,
Zue diner Muetter Anne.
Si git dir Chäs und Brod,
's isch besser as der bitter Tod.   (R., p. 464.)

H

" Gold-chafer, up and away, up to thy high story, to thy
Mother Anne, who gives thee bread and cheese. 'Tis better
than bitter death."

In Swabia they sing :—

> Sonnevögele flieg aus,
> Flieg in meiner Ahne Haus,
> Bring mir Aepfel und Bire ;
> Komm bald wieder. (Me., p. 24.)

" Sunbird, fly away, fly to my ancestress' house ; bring
me apples and pears ; come back soon."

This request to the ladybird to bring down
gifts from heaven has a parallel in our rhyme
which entreats it to "carry up ten pounds, and
bring down eleven."

According to another of our rhymes the one
who is safe at home is Tom, who lies under the
grindelstone, that is the grindstone. The analysis of the stories that are told of Tom shows
that he is related to the northern god Thor, and
that the grindstone corresponds to Thor's hammer.
Moreover, in Scandinavian folk-lore there is a
house-sprite called Tommelgubbe, literally Tom-
boy, who took offence if work was done on a
Thursday, the day sanctified to the god Thor.
The hammer of Thor was called *Mjölnir*, that is

pounder, and with it the god was busy in summer-time in heaven, pounding ice into snow.

In an old story-book called *Tom Hickathrift*, otherwise *Hickifric*,[1] traits are preserved in connection with Tom, which recall the peculiarities of the god Thor. Tom dwelt with his mother, who slept on straw; there was no father. Thor had no father; his mother was designated as Godmor. Tom ate hugely, Thor did the same. Tom flung his hammer into the river, Thor measured distance by throwing his hammer. Tom carted beer—a trait that recalls Thor's fits of drunkenness. On one occasion Tom made himself a weapon by sticking an axle-tree into a waggon-wheel, which suggests that Thor's hammer was a flat stone mace. Likewise Tom, having broken his club, " seized upon a lusty raw-boned miller," and used him as a weapon. Can we hesitate from accepting that this " miller" in a confused manner recalls the *Mjölnir*—that is the hammer—of the northern god Thor ?

The analysis of the ladybird rhymes takes us even farther afield. In Saxony they sing :—

[1] Reprinted Halliwell, 1849, p. 81 ff.

Flieg, Käfer, flieg, dein Vater ist im Krieg,
Deine Mutter ist in den Stiefel gekroche,
Hat das linke Bein gebroche.

(M., p. 347.)

"Fly, chafer, fly, father has gone to war, mother has crept into the shoe, she has broken her left leg."

The mother with the broken leg of this rhyme recalls the limping mother of the Babyland game, and the person in *Drop Handkerchief*, who was bitten. The expression of "creeping into a shoe" yields a clue to the nature of the woman of one of our rhymes who lived in a shoe, and was oppressed by the number of her children. In one form this rhyme, cited above in connection with the tale of Mother Hubbard, describes how the children were to all appearance dead, but were quickened into life. This conception is allied to the quickening into life of the babes in the Babyland game. In its earliest printed form the rhyme stands as follows :—

There was an old woman who lived in a shoe,
She had so many children she didn't know what to do ;
She gave them some broth without any bread,
She whipped all their bums and sent them to bed.

(c. 1783, p. 52.)

Those of our ladybird rhymes which call on the insect in matters of love divination have their closest parallels in Scandinavia. In Sweden they sing :—

> Jungfru Marias Nyckelpiga,
> Flyg öster, flyg vester,
> Flyg dit der bor din älskede.   (1849, p. 5.)

"Fly, Our Lady's keybearer! fly east, fly west, fly where thy lover dwells."

Of the rhymes of this class, one introduces the term Golloway. This may be intended for Yellow Way, the course of the sun in daytime, as distinct from the Milky Way, the course of the stars at night.

Another rhyme begins with the call Bishop, bishop, which has puzzled various commentators. I venture to suggest that the word be read Bee-ship, and that it indicates the boat that sailed across heaven bearing the souls of the dead, who were figured as bees. For the spirits of those who passed away, viewed under one aspect, were bees, and the ship that conveyed the dead in Norsk saga was actually designated as the *Bÿskip*. Mannhardt, in illustration, cites a

line which the skald Egil Skallagrimssonr, whose
date is between 902 and 980, sang on his son
that had been drowned :—

> Byrr es bȳskips i boe kominn kvanar son.

"In the beeship there has gone the son of my wife."

Our commentators inaccurately translate the
expression as "City of the Hive" (C. P., I,
546).

According to a fancy of the Welsh bards,
Britain was peopled with bees before the arrival
of man, and this was held to account for its name,
the "Isle of Honey."

A Prussian ladybird rhyme also mentions the
boat that sailed across heaven.   In Dantzig they
sing :—

> Herrgotspferdchen, fliege weg,
> Dein Häuschen brennt, dein Kähnchen schwimmt,
> Deine Kinder schreien nach Butterbrod ;
> Herrgotspferdchen, fliege weg.   (M., 349.)

"God Almighty's little horse, fly away, thy house is on
fire, thy boat is afloat, thy children cry for bread and
butter."

From an early period the sun was supposed to
be conveyed in a boat, and boats were associated

with divinities half the world over. Tacitus was acquainted with the boat of the goddess Isis that was conveyed about in Alexandria, and he described the boat that was taken about in procession by the heathen Germans in their cult of Hertha, as the boat of Isis (Gr., p. 214). The sun-boat of Ra in Egypt conveyed the dead to heaven. So did the golden ship of Odin in Scandinavia, which conveyed the bodies of the fallen warriors to Valhalla. The remembrance of this sun-boat probably gave rise to the story how Ikaros invented sails. It may linger still in the "beeship" of our rhymes, and in the "Kähnchen" of the corresponding German lady-bird rhyme.

CHAPTER X

RIDDLE-RHYMES

AMONG other rhymes which date some way back in history are those which may fitly be called riddle-rhymes. Some of these have close parallels in the nursery lore of other countries. The most interesting example of this class is the rhyme on Humpty-Dumpty which deals with the egg. The egg from the earliest times formed an enigma in itself, and was looked upon as representing the origin of life. Aristophanes knew of the great bird that laid the world-egg. According to *Kalevala*, the Finnish epic, the world-egg fell and broke. Its upper part became the vault of heaven, its lower part the earth. The yolk formed the sun, the white the moon, and the fragments of the shell became the stars in heaven. Reminiscences of this idea of a world-egg linger in the *Senchus Mor* of Ireland and in the *Volospa*

of Norse saga. In Tibet the holy Budh is
represented holding in his hand a broken egg-shell,
on the edge of which a diminutive human being
is sometimes represented sitting. These world-
wide conceptions account for the existence of
numerous riddles that are current about the egg.

The rhyme on Humpty-Dumpty among us is
current in three variations :—

> Humpty-Dumpty sate on a wall,
> Humpty-Dumpty had a great fall ;
> Threescore men and threescore more
> Cannot place Humpty-Dumpty as he was before.
>
> (1810, p. 36.)
>
> Humpty-Dumpty sate on a wall,
> Humpty-Dumpty had a great fall ;
> All the king's soldiers and all the king's men
> Cannot set Humpty-Dumpty up again.
>
> (1842, p. 113.)
>
> Humpty-Dumpty lay in a beck
> With all his sinews around his neck ;
> Forty doctors and forty wights
> Couldn't put Humpty-Dumpty to rights.
>
> (1846, p. 209.)

Many parallels of this rhyme were collected
from different parts of Europe by Mannhardt.
In these Humpty-Dumpty appears under various
names. They include Hümpelken-Pümpelken,

Rüntzelken-Püntzelken,Wirgele-Wargele, Gigele-
Gagele, and Etje-Papetje in different parts of
Germany, and Lille-Trille and Lille Bulle in
Scandinavia. The closest parallel of our rhyme
hails from Saxony, and stands as follows :—

> Hümpelken-Pümpelken sat up de Bank,
> Hümpelken-Pümpelken fēl von de Bank ;
> Do is kēn Docter in Engelland
> De Hümpelken-Pümpelken kurere kann.
>
> (M., p. 416.)[1]

"H.-P. sat on a bench, H.-P. fell from the bench ;
there is no doctor in Engelland who can restore H.-P."

In Switzerland the rhyme of Humpty-Dumpty
is told of Annebadadeli. The usual answer is
an egg, but sometimes it is an icicle or a feeding-
bottle.

In Scandinavia they say :—

> Lille Bulle trilla' ner a skulle ;
> Ingen man i detta lan'
> Lille Bulle laga kan.   (1849, p. 9.)

"Little B. fell from the shelf, no man in the whole
land can restore little B."

This has a further parallel in France in a rhyme

[1] Cf. also Mannhardt, *Das Rätsel vom Ei*, in *Zeitschrift
für deutsche Mythologie*, IV, 1859, p. 394 ff.

which reproduces the German expression Engelland regardless of its intrinsic meaning :—

> Boule, boule su l'keyere,
> Boule, boule par terre.
> Y n'a nuz homme en Angleterre
> Pou l'erfaire.[1]

"B. b. on the bench, B. b. on the ground. There is
no man in England who can restore him."

The forty doctors of our rhyme who figure also
as twice threescore men, reappear in the German
rhyme as "no doctor in *Engelland*," as "no man
in all the land" in the Scandinavian rhyme, and
as "no man in England" literally translated, of
the French version.

In one version of our rhyme those who are
powerless to restore what is broken are described
as "all the king's soldiers and all the king's men."
This expression is also used in the riddle-rhymes
on Smoke and on the Well, which are found in
our own and in foreign nursery collections.

> As round as an apple, as deep as a cup,
> And all the king's horses cannot pull it up.
>   (The Well, 1846, p. 75.)

[1] Rolland, E., *Devinettes on énigmes populaires*, 1877,
p. 199, from Mons.

> As high as a castle, as weak as a wastle,
> And all the king's soldiers cannot pull it down.
>
> (Smoke, 1849, p. 144.)

In Swabia they say :—

> Es ist etwas in meinem Haus,
> Es ziehen es hundert tausend Gäule nicht naus.
>
> (Me., p. 79.)

"There is something in my house, not a hundred thousand horses can pull it out."

The answer is "Smoke." In France they say :—

> Qu'est-ce-qui est rond comme un dé,
> Et que des chevaux ne peuvent porter.[1]

"What is as round as a thimble, and horses cannot pull it?"

The answer is "A well." Possibly the "king" of these rhymes stands for the sun as the representative of power, whose horses and men are alike powerless.

The egg, which in these rhymes is designated by fanciful names, in other riddle-rhymes current abroad is described as a cask containing two kinds of beer. A riddle was put by the god Wodan in the character of a wayfarer to King Heidrek, and stood as follows :—

[1] Rolland, E., *Devinettes on énigmes populaires*, 1877, p. 98, from Paris.

"Blond - haired brides, bondswomen both, carried ale to the barn ; the casks were not turned with hands nor forged by hammer ; she that made it strutted about outside the isle." The answer is "Eider-ducks' eggs" (C. P., I, 89).

The egg is also likened to a cask containing beer in a short riddle-rhyme which is current from Lapland to Hungary. In the Faroe Islands it takes this form : "Bolli fell from the ledge, all its hoops fell off. There is no man in the East, there is no man in the West, who can restore it" (M., p. 417). In Prussia they say :—

> Kommt ein Tonn aus Engelland,
> Ohne Boden, ohne Band ;
> Ist zweierleai Bier drin. (Sim., p. 287.)

"A cask comes from Engelland, without bottom, without band ; it contains two kinds of beer."

Among ourselves there is no riddle-rhyme, as far as I know, which describes the egg as a cask containing beer. But in the seventeenth century the word Humpty-Dumpty was used to designate a drink which consisted of ale boiled in brandy,[1] and this conception obviously hangs together with

[1] Murray's Dictionary : *Humpty-Dumpty,*

the two kinds of beer of the foreign riddle-rhymes on the egg.

Other riddle-rhymes current among ourselves or abroad describe the egg as a house or a castle. The following one describes it as an enigma in itself:—

> As I was going o'er London Bridge
> I saw something under a hedge ;
> 'Twas neither fish, flesh, fowl, nor bone,
> And yet in three weeks it runned alone.
>
> (1846, p. 213.)

Girls in America play a game called *Humpty-Dumpty*. They sit on the ground with their skirts tightly gathered around them so as to enclose the feet. The leader begins some rhyme, all join in, and at a certain word previously agreed upon, all throw themselves backwards, keeping their skirts tightly grasped. The object is to recover the former position without letting go the skirt (N., p. 132).

Possibly the game is older than the riddle-rhymes, for these rhymes describe *Humpty-Dumpty* as sitting on a wall, or a bank, or a ledge, or as lying in a beck, which for an actual egg are impossible situations. They are intelligible on the assumption that the sport is older than the rhyme, and that the rhyme describes human beings who are personating eggs.

The name Humpty-Dumpty itself is one of the large class of rhyming compounds which are formed by the varied reduplication of the same word. Perhaps they originally conveyed a definite meaning. The word Humpty-Dumpty is allied to *hump* and to *dump*, words which express round-ness and shortness. Another name of the kind is Hoddy-Doddy, which occurs in the following riddle-rhyme :—

> Hoddy-Doddy with a round, black body ;
> Three legs and a wooden hat, what is that?
>
> (1849, p. 142.)

The answer is " An iron pot." [1] The word Hoddy-Doddy in the sixteenth century was directly used to express " a short and dumpy person " (1553). It was also applied to a " hen-pecked man " (1598). [2] The meaning of shortness and roundness is expressed also by the name of the foreign equivalents of Humpty-Dumpty. The

[1] A workman in Berkshire in 1905 repeated this riddle to H. P.

[2] Murray's Dictionary : *Hoddy-Doddy*.

German Hümpelken-Pümpelken, and probably Lille Bulle of Scandinavia convey the same idea. On the other hand, the names Wirgele-Wargele and Gigele - Gagele suggest instability. The Danish Lille Trille is allied to *lille trölle*, little troll, that is, a member of the earlier and stumpy race of men who, by a later age, were accounted dwarves. These were credited in folk-lore with sex-relations of a primitive kind, an allusion to which seems to linger in the word Hoddy-Doddy as applied to a hen-pecked man.

Among other rhyming compounds is the word *Hitty-Pitty*. It occurs in a riddle-rhyme which Halliwell traced back to the seventeenth century (MS. Harl. 1962) :—

> Hitty Pitty within the wall,
> Hitty Pitty without the wall ;
> If you touch Hitty Pitty,
> Hitty Pitty will bite you.
>
> (A nettle, 1849, p. 149.)

This verse is sometimes used in playing *Hide and Seek* as a warning to the player who approaches the place that is "hot" (1894, I, 211). A variation of the word is *Highty-Tighty*, which is preserved in the following rhyme :—

Highty, tighty, paradighty, clothed in green,
The king could not read it, no more could the queen ;
They sent for a wise man out of the East,
Who said it had horns, but was not a beast.

(1842, p. 118.)

The answer is " A holly tree."

Another rhyming compound is preserved in the
riddle-rhyme on the sunbeam :—

Hick-a-more, Hack-a-more
Hung on a kitchen door ;
Nothing so long, and nothing so strong,
As Hick-a-more, Hack-a-more
Hung on the kitchen door.   (1846, p. 207.)

The following riddle-rhyme preserves the word
lilly-low, which is the north-country term for the
flame of a candle :—

Lilly-low, lilly-low, set up on end,
See little baby go out at town end.

(A candle, 1849, p. 146.)

Another riddle on the candle, which also stands
in MS. Harl. 1962, and has found its way into
nursery collections, is :—

Little Nancy Etticoat with a white petticoat,
And a red nose ;
The longer she stands, the shorter she grows.

(1842, p. 114.)

I

This recalls a riddle current in Devonshire, where the sky is called widdicote :—

> Widdicote, widdicote, over cote hang ;
> Nothing so broad, and nothing so lang
> As Widdicote, etc.   (1892, p. 333.)

All these riddle-rhymes are based on primitive conceptions, and all have parallels in the nursery lore of other countries. The rhyme on Hoddy-Doddy in Norwegian is simply descriptive ; in France it is told in the form of words exchanged between *Noiret*, "Blacky," the pot, and *Rouget*, "Ruddy," the fire. In Italy the Pot, the Smoke, and the Fire are described as three sisters. Again, the riddle-rhyme on the candle is told in Swabia and in France. But in no case are the foreign parallels as close as in the riddle-rhyme of Humpty-Dumpty, and in no case do they preserve the same interesting allusions.

CHAPTER XI

CUMULATIVE PIECES

WE now turn to rhymes which dwell on different ideas and present life under other aspects. In these rhymes there is much on spells, on the magic properties of numbers, and on sacrificial hunting. A fatalistic tendency underlies many of these rhymes, and there are conscious efforts to avert danger.

The different range of ideas which are here expressed is reflected in the form of verse in which they are presented. While the rhymes hitherto discussed are set in verse which depends for its consistency on tail rhyme and assonance, the pieces that deal with the magic properties of things and with hunting, are mostly set in a form of verse that depends for its consistency on repetition and cumulation. This difference in form is probably due to the different

115

origin of these pieces.   Rhymed verse may have originated in dancing and singing—cumulative verse in recitation and instruction.

In cumulative recitation one sentence is uttered and repeated, a second sentence is uttered and repeated, then the first sentence is said; a third sentence is uttered and repeated, followed by the second and the first.   Thus each sentence adds to the piece and carries it back to the beginning.   Supposing each letter to stand for a sentence, the form of recitation can thus be described : A, a ; B, b, a ; C, c, b, a ; D, d, c, b, a ; etc.   This manner of recitation is well known among ourselves, but I know of no word to designate it.   In Brittany the form of recitation is known as *chant de grénouille*, i.e. frog-chant. A game of forfeits was known in the eighteenth century, which was called *The Gaping Wide-mouthed Waddling Frog*, in which the verses were recited in exactly the same manner.   We shall return to it later.   A relation doubtless exists between this game and the French expression frog-chant.

Among our most familiar pieces that are set in

cumulative form are *The Story of the Old Woman and Her Pig* and *This is the House that Jack built*. They both consist of narrative, and are told as stories. *This is the House that Jack built* first appeared in print as a toy-book that was issued by Marshall at his printing office, Aldermary Churchyard. It is illustrated with cuts, and its date is about 1770. Perhaps the story is referred to in the *Boston News Letter* (No. 183) of 12–19 April, 1739, in which the reviewer of Tate and Brady's Version of the Psalms remarks that this "makes our children think of the tune of their vulgar playsong so like it: this is the man all forlorn." The sentence looks like a variation of the line " this is the maiden all forlorn " in *This is the House that Jack built.*

In 1819 there was published in London a satire by Hone, called *The Political House that Jack built*. It was illustrated by Cruikshank, and went through fifty-four editions. In form it imitates the playsong, which was doubtless as familiar then as it is now.

The playsong in the form published by Marshall begins :—

This is the house that Jack built,—
This is the malt that lay in the house that Jack built,—
This is the rat that ate the malt that lay in the house that
    Jack built,—

which is followed by the cat that killed the rat—
the dog that worried the cat—the cow that tossed
the dog—the maiden that milked the cow—the
man that kissed the maid—the priest that married
them. Here it ended. But a further line added
by Halliwell (1842, p. 222) mentioned the cock
that crowed on the morn of the wedding-day, and
a lady of over seventy has supplied me with one
more line, on the knife that killed the cock. She
tells me that she had the story from her nurse,
and that she does not remember seeing it in
print. The version she repeated in cumulative
form, told to me, ended as follows:—

> This is the knife with a handle of horn,
> that killed the cock that crowed in the morn,
> that wakened the priest all shaven and shorn,
> that married the man all tattered and torn,
> unto the maiden all forlorn,
> that milked the cow with a crumpled horn,
> that tossed the dog over the barn,
> that worried the cat that killed the rat
> that ate the malt that lay in the house
> that Jack built.

The greater part of this piece consists of rhymed verse, and deals with matters of courtship. The idea of a cock sacrificed on the wedding-day is certainly heathen in origin, but its introduction forms a new departure when we come to compare this piece with its foreign parallels and with the story of *The Old Woman and Her Pig*. These pieces are all set in the same form, and all introduce a regular sequence of relative powers.

The Old Woman and Her Pig was first printed by Halliwell (1842, p. 219). It tells how the woman found sixpence, and how she set out for market, and bought a pig which on the way back refused to jump over the stile. In order to break the spell that had fallen on it, she summoned to her aid: dog—stick—fire—water—ox—butcher—rope—rat—cat—cow. The cow finally gave the milk required by the cat, which set the other powers going, and thus enabled the woman to get home that night. Halliwell was impressed by the antiquity of this sequence, and included in his collection a translation of a Hebrew chant which has considérable likeness to the tale of *The Old*

Woman and Her Pig.   This chant is told in the first person.   It begins :—

> A kid, a kid my father bought
> For two pieces of money,
> > A kid, a kid.
>
> Then came the cat and ate the kid,
> That my father bought,
> For two pieces of money.
> > A kid, a kid.
> > > (1842, p. 6.)

It further introduces dog—staff—fire—water—ox—butcher—angel of death—Holy One.

The Hebrew chant of the kid was printed in Venice as far back as 1609, and was made the subject of the learned Latin dissertation *De Haedo* by Probst von der Hardt in 1727 (R., p. 153). It was again discussed by P. N. Leberecht in 1731.[1] The chant forms part of the Jewish liturgy, and is still recited in the original Hebrew or in the vernacular as part of a religious ceremonial at Easter. Opinions on the origin and the meaning of the chant differ. One learned rabbi interpreted it as setting forth how each

---

[1] The article by Leberecht is in *Der Christliche Reformator*, Leipzig, 1731, XVII, 28.

power in creation is kept within bounds by a power that stands above it. It teaches how he who goes wrong is at the mercy of one stronger than himself. But according to another interpretation the Father who bought the kid was Jehovah himself, the kid was the Hebrew, the cat represented the Assyrians, the dog the Babylonians, and so forth ; and the whole poem described the position of the Jews at the time of the Crusades.

The Hebrew chant and its relation to *The Old Woman and her Pig* engaged the attention of Professor Tylor, who remarked on the solemn ending of the Hebrew chant, which according to him may incline us to think that we really have before us this composition in something like its first form. "If so," he says, "then it follows that our familiar tale of the Old Woman who couldn't get the kid (*or* pig) over the stile, must be considered as a broken-down adaptation of this old Jewish poem."[1]

But the tale of the Old Woman taken in conjunction with *This is the House that Jack built* and its numerous foreign parallels, shows

[1] Tylor, E. B., *Primitive Culture*, II, 86.

that these sequences of relative powers, far from being broken-down adaptations, are at least as meaningful as the Hebrew chant.   For the underlying conception in all cases is that a spell has fallen on an object which man is appropriating to his use.   The spell extends to everything, be it man or beast, that comes within the range of its influence, and the unmaking of the spell necessitates going back step by step to the point at which it originated.

Halliwell compared a piece current in Denmark with *This is the House that Jack built* :—

> Der har du det haus som Jacob bygde.
>
> "Here hast thou the house that Jacob built."[1]

Many other versions of this tale are current in Germany and Scandinavia.   In them it is sometimes a question of a house, sometimes of corn, oftenest of cutting oats or of garnering pears. The cumulative form is throughout adhered to. One German piece called *Ist alles verlorn*, "all is lost," begins :—

---

[1] Halliwell, 1849, p. 6, citing Thiele, II, 3, 146.   I cannot find this book.

Es kam eine Maus gegangen
In unser Kornehaŭs,
Die nahm das Korn gefangen,
In ŭnserm Kornehaŭs.
Die Maus das Korn,
Ist alles verlorn
In ŭnserm Kornehaŭs.   (Sim., p. 256.)

"There came a mouse into our corn-house, she seized the corn in our corn-house. The mouse, the corn, now all is lost in our corn-house."

The other powers are rat, cat, fox, wolf, bear, man, maid. This piece, like *This is the House that Jack built*, ends abruptly.

Among the less primitive variations of the tale is one recorded in Sonneberg (S., p. 102), and another in the north of France, which both substitute the name of Peter for that of Jack, that is a Christian name for a heathen one. In France the piece is called *La Mouche*, literally "the fly," but its contents indicate that not *mouche* but the Latin *mus* (mouse) was originally meant. The tale departs from the usual form, and has a refrain :—

Voici la maison que Pierre a bâtie,
Il sortait un rat de sa raterie,
Qui fit rentrer la mouch' dans sa moucherie :

Rat à mouche,
Belle, belle mouche
Jamais je n'ai vu si belle mouche.

(D.B., p. 116.)

"This is the house that Peter built. A rat came out of a rat-hole, and made the fly go into the fly-hole. Rat to fly, lovely fly, never saw I so lovely a fly."

The other powers are dog, bear, man, maid, abbot, pope, devil.

The same tale is told in Austria (V., p. 113), and in Prussia (F., p. 197), where it is called *Das Haus vom hölzernen Mann*, "the house of the wooden Man." In Prussia it is recited as a game of forfeits. The sequence of the powers in the one version is house, door, lock, band, mouse, cat, dog, stick, fire, water, ox, butcher, devil; and in the other, house, door, lock, band, mouse, cat, huntsman.

Jack in Germany is called Jockel, Jöggeli, Jokele. *The Master who sent out Jockel* is mentioned already in the Gargantua of Fischart, which was published in 1575 (Chap. xxv.). The name Jack among ourselves is applied to a person or an object of peculiar serviceableness, as in Jack-of-all-trades, or boot-jack. But in Germany the expression "to send Jockel on an errand" implies that this will never get done.

In Vogtland the current nursery version of this piece begins :—

> Es schickt der Herr den Gôkel 'naus,
> Er soll den Haber schneiden.   (Du., p. 35.)

"The master sent out Gokel to cut oats."

As he failed to come back, dog, fire, water, ox, butcher, hangman, devil, were sent after him.

In Swabia Jokele (Br., p. 44), and in Switzerland Joggeli, was sent to knock off pears on which a spell had fallen. The chant in Zürich has been traced back to the year 1769, and it begins :—

> Es ist ein Baam im Gärtle hinne,
> d' Birren wänd nüd fallen.
> Do schückt de Bur de Joggeli usen
> Er soll di Birren schütteln.   (R., p. 155.)

"There is a tree in the garden, its pears will not drop. The peasant sent out Joggeli to knock them off."

But the pears refused to be knocked off, and the usual sequence of powers was sent to secure them.

The tale of Jack was current in Münster in Westphalia also, where it was taken over by the

Church, and annually recited at the religious procession which took place on the eve of the feast of St. Lambert, 17 September. This was done as late as the year 1810 (R., p. 155). The recitation was followed or accompanied by a dance, the purpose of which is not recorded. Perhaps the procession stood in relation to the actual garnering of pears, and the tale was recited in order to secure a good harvest. In this case not Jack, but *der Jäger*, "the huntsman," was dispatched to knock the pears off, and the sequence of powers included dog, stick, fire, water, calf, butcher, hangman, devil.

This adoption by the Church of the sequence of powers shows that we have to do with the remains of a heathen ritual, which found its way into a Christian celebration, as the tale of the kid found its way into the Easter celebration of the Jewish Church. In both instances the sequence of relative powers is preserved, and in both it is question of making an object secure for the use of man.

The same sequence of powers is preserved also in the traditional game that is known as *Dump*

among ourselves (1894, I, 117; II, 419), and
as *Club Fist* in America (N., p. 134).   In this
game it is also a question of building a house,
and of knocking off pears.   The action of the
players, however, stands in no obvious relation to
the words that are used.   Sometimes three, sometimes a number of lads, crowd together and place
their fists sideways one on the other, till they
form a pile of clenched hands.   The last boy, who
has a fist free, knocks off the fists one by one,
saying :—

> (In Yorkshire) What's this ?—(Answer) Dump.
> (In America) What's that?—(Answer) A pear.
> Take it off or I'll knock it off.

In Shropshire all sing together :—

> I've built my house, I've built my wall;
> I don't care where my chimneys fall.

When all the fists are knocked down, the
following dialogue ensues :—

What's there?—Cheese and bread and a mouldy half-
penny.
Where's my share?—I put it on the shelf, and the cat
got it.
Where's the cat ?— She's run nine miles through the wood.
Where's the wood?—T' fire burnt it.

Where's the fire ?—T' water sleckt it.
Where's the water ?—T' ox drunk it.
Where's the ox ?—T' butcher killed 'em.
Where's the butcher?—Upon the church-top cracking
    nuts, and you may go and eat the shells ; and *them
    as* speak first shall have nine nips, nine scratches,
    and nine boxes on the ear.   (1849, p. 128.)

Silence falls, all try not to laugh, and he who
first allows a word to escape him, is punished by
the others in the methods adopted by schoolboys.
In the Scottish game the punishment is described
as "nine nips, nine nobs, nine double douncornes,
and a good blow on the back."

In France the same game is known as *Le Pied
de Bœuf*, "the foot of the ox," and a scramble
of fists starts at the words :—

Neuf, je tiens mon pied de bœuf.   (Mo., p. 351.)
    "Nine, 1 hold my ox's foot";

the number nine in this case being also mentioned.

The meting out of punishments by nines goes far
back in history. It was associated with a Yule-tide
sport which is still practised in Denmark and in
Schleswig, and is known as *Ballerrune* or *Balder-
rune*. Every member of the assembled company

repeated a formula on "Balder Rune and his wife," and he who made a mistake received nine blows, as in our game.   The custom was explained by the legend that the god Balder, incensed at his wife's loquacity, chastised her by giving her nine blows, and ordered that this should be repeated every year, so that women be reminded that it is their duty to be silent when their husbands speak (H., p. 44).

In the game of *Dump* also, it is the person who speaks first that is punished, but there is nothing to suggest that this was a woman, for the game is essentially a boys' game.

The story of *The Woman and her Pig* (*or Kid*), like that of Jack, is told over a wide geographical area.   In the Scottish version the woman lived in a wee house and found two pennies and bought a kid.   On coming home she saw a bush and wished to pull off its berries, and could not.   She set the kid to watch the house, and went to seek the help of dog, stick, fire, water, ox, axe, smith, rope, mouse, cat, milk, in her hope of breaking the spell that had fallen on the bush.   Each animal or object refused " to do the next one

K

harm, saying that it never did it any harm
itself"; but the cat finally could not resist the
temptation of lapping the milk (1870, p. 57).
Thus the tale introduced a moral element which
is not found elsewhere.

In Sweden the tale of *The Old Woman and her
Pig* is called *Konen och Grisen Fick*, "the woman
and her pig Fick," and the pig refused to leave
off eating acorns. A similar tale is called *Gossen
och Geten Näppa*, "the lad and the kid Näppa,"
(1849, p. 6). In Elsass the pig is called *Schnirrchele*
(St., p. 93), in Transylvania it is *Mischka* or
Bitschki (Sch., p. 372). And a version from the
north of France tells how *Biquette* got into a
cabbage-patch from which stick, fire, water, were
summoned to expel her. *Biquette* is described as
a kid (D., p. 122). In Languedoc *Biquette* reappears as *Bouquaire-Bouquil*, who is furnished
with horns and does havoc in a millet-field from
which he is expelled with the help of wolf, dog,
stick, fire, water, ox, rope (M. L., p. 538). In all
cases the animal is one that is provided with
horns. Millet is one of the oldest cereals that
were cultivated in Europe, the displacement of

which by the cultivation of corn had begun in England when Pytheas visited these shores in the fourth century B.C. Can the " malt" of *This is the House that Jack built* stand for millet?

A French piece is current in Remiremont which is called *Le Conjurateur et le Loup*, " the magician and the wolf." It describes the contest between them, and shows that the making and unmaking of spells is involved :—

> 'y a un loup dedans le bois,
> Le loup ne veut pas sortir du bois.
> Ha, j' te promets, compèr' Brocard,
> Tu sortiras de ce lieu-là.   (R., p. 152.)

"There is a wolf in the wood, the wolf will not come out of the wood. Ha, I promise you, brother Brocard, you will soon come out."

And the magician summons to his assistance stick, fire, water, calf, butcher, devil, which help him to expel the wolf.

Even more primitive than this tale is one current in Languedoc, in which a spell has fallen on a root or turnip, which is finally raised by the hog. It begins: "The old woman went into the garden in order to pull out a turnip.

When the old man saw that the old woman did not come back, he went into the garden and saw the old woman pulling at the turnip. The old man pulled at the old woman, the old woman pulled at the turnip, but the turnip stuck fast." They were followed by daughter-in-law, son, man, maid, and so forth, including the cat and the rat. Finally the hog came to the rescue. Instead of pulling like the others, he attacked the turnip from below, and by doing so he succeeded in raising it, otherwise the spell would continue, "and the root would still be holding fast" (M. I.., p. 541).

The comparison of these various tales or pieces shows that dog, stick, fire, water, ox, butcher, form a sequence of powers that was accepted over a wide geographical area. They were invoked wherever it was question of breaking a spell that had fallen on a coveted object, the object including pigs, pears, oats, berries, millet, and roots. These are products that were prized in Europe from a remote period in antiquity. As the products are primitive, so probably is the form of verse in which the story is told of their being made fast.   For the same form of verse is used in a further class of pieces to which we now turn, and which, by their contents, betray a pre-Christian origin.

CHAPTER XII

CHANTS OF NUMBERS

AMONG our traditional games, some consist of a dialogue in which the answer is set in cumulative form. These include the game known as *The Twelve Days of Christmas*, which was played on Twelfth-Day night by the assembled company before eating mince-pies and twelfth cake. In the game of *Twelve Days* each player in succession repeated the gifts of the day, and raised his fingers and hand according to the number which he named. Each answer included the one that had gone before, and forfeits were paid for each mistake that was made. (1894, II, 315.)

The oldest printed version of the words used in playing *Twelve Days* stands in one of the diminutive toy-books exhibited at South Kensington Museum by E. Pearson. These words begin :—

The first day of Christmas, my true love gave me
A partridge in a pear-tree.
The second day of Christmas, my true love gave me
Two turtle-doves and a partridge in a pear-tree.

And so forth, enumerating three French hens, four colly birds, five gold rings, six geese a-laying, seven swans a-swimming, eight maids a-milking, nine drummers drumming, ten pipers piping, eleven ladies dancing, twelve lords leaping.

The same game is played in Scotland, where it is known as *The Yule Days,* but is carried on to thirteen.

The king sent his lady on the first Yule day
A papingo-aye [i.e. peacock or parrot]
Who learns my carol and carries it away?
The king sent his lady on the second Yule day
Two partridges and a papingo-aye.

(1870, p. 42.)

On the third day he sent three plovers; on the fourth, a goose that was grey; on the fifth, three starlings; on the sixth, three goldspinks; on the seventh, a bull that was brown; on the eighth, three ducks a-merry laying; on the ninth, three swans a-merry swimming; on the tenth, an Arabian baboon; on the eleventh, three hinds a-merry dancing; on the twelfth, two maids a-merry dancing; on the thirteenth three stalks of corn.

In Cambresis, in the North of France, the same game is called *Les dons de l'an*, "the gifts of the year," but the gifts correspond in number with the number of the day. They are : one partridge, two turtle-doves, three wood-pigeons, four ducks flying, five rabbits trotting, six hares a-field, seven hounds running, eight shorn sheep, nine horned oxen, ten good turkeys, eleven good hams, twelve small cheeses (D. B., II, 125).

In the West of France the piece is described as a song. It is called *La foi de la loi*, that is, "the creed of authority," and is sung *avec solennité*. It begins :—

> La premièr' parti' d'la foi de la loi,
> Dit' la moi, frère Grégoire.
> —Un bon farci sans os—
> La deuxième parti' d'la foi de la loi,
> Dit' le moi, frère Grégoire
> —Deux ventres de veau,
> Un bon farci sans os. (B., II, 271.)

"The first part of the creed of authority, tell it me, Brother Gregory. A good stuffing without bones. The second part of the creed of authority . . . two breasts of veal."

And so forth, enumerating three joints of beef, four pig's trotters, five legs of mutton, six partridges with cabbage, seven spitted rabbits, eight plates of salad, nine plates of (? *chapitre*), ten full casks, eleven beautiful full-breasted maidens, twelve knights with their rapiers.

The same conceptions underlie a Languedoc chant, in which the numbers are, however, carried on to fifteen. The gifts in this case are made on the first fifteen days of the month of May :—

> Le prumiè del més de mai,
> Qu' embouiarei à mai mio.
> Uno perdic que bolo, que bolo.

> (M. L., p. 486.)

" The first of the month of May, what shall I send to my lady love ?—A partridge that flies and flies."

And similarly we read of two doves, three white pigeons, four ducks flying in the air, five rabbits, six hares, seven hunting dogs, eight white horses, nine horned oxen, ten bleating sheep, eleven soldiers coming from war, twelve maidens, thirteen white nosegays, fourteen white loaves, fifteen casks of wine.

The contents of these chants at first sound like

nonsense, but on looking at them more closely one notes that the gifts which they enumerate mostly consist of birds and beasts that are conceived as food. We know that the weather on Twelve Days was carefully observed, since the weather of the months of the ensuing year was prognosticated from that of the corresponding day of the twelve.[1] A like conception perhaps underlies these enumerations of food, which may refer to the representative sports of the months.

The game of *Twelve Days* in a degraded form is known as *The Gaping Wide-mouthed Waddling Frog*, in which the crux likewise consists of answering the question with rapidity and exactness. But words are purposely chosen that are difficult to enunciate and to remember. The result is a string of nonsense. The words used in playing *The Gaping Wide-mouthed Waddling Frog* were first printed in a toy-book of the eighteenth century. Persons who are still living remember it in this form as a Christmas game. As in playing *Twelve Days*, the players sat in

[1] Frazer, loc. cit., 1900, p. 143 ; Rolland, *Almanach des traditions populaires*, 1883, Jan. 1–12.

a circle, a dialogue ensued, and the answers were given in cumulative form. He who made a mistake gave a forfeit.

> Buy this of me :—What is it?
> The gaping wide-mouthed waddling frog.
>
> Buy this of me :—What is it?
> Two pudding ends will choke a dog,
> With a gaping wide-mouthed waddling frog.
>
> Buy this of me :—What is it?
> Three monkeys tied to a clog,
> Two pudding ends will choke a dog, etc.

The answer to the last question stood as follows :—

Twelve huntsmen with horns and hounds,
Hunting over other men's grounds ;
Eleven ships sailing o'er the main,
Some bound for France and some for Spain,
I wish them all safe home again ;
Ten comets in the sky,
Some low and some high ;
Nine peacocks in the air,
I wonder how they all came there,
I do not know and I don't care ;
Eight joiners in joiner's hall
Working with their tools and all.
Seven lobsters in a dish,
As fresh as any heart could wish ;
Six beetles against the wall [*or* six spiders in the wall],
Close by an old woman's apple stall ;

> Five puppies by our bitch Ball
> Who daily for their breakfast call ;
> Four horses stuck in a bog ;
> Three monkeys tied to a clog ;
> Two pudding ends would choke a dog ;
> With a gaping wide-mouthed waddling frog.

Many rhymes that originated in these nonsense verses have found their way into nursery collections.   Halliwell printed the following lines as a separate nursery rhyme :—

> Eight ships on the main,
> I wish them all safe back again ;
> Seven eagles in the air,
> I wonder how they all came there ;
> I don't know, nor I don't care.
> Six spiders on the wall,
> Close to an old woman's apple stall ;
> Five puppies in Highga e hall,
> Who daily for their breakfast call ;
> Four mares stuck in a bog,
> Three monkeys tied to a log,
> Two pudding ends will choke a dog,
> With a gaping wide mouthed waddling frog.
>
> (1842, p. 246.)

Halliwell also printed some utterly debased rhymes, in which, however, numbers are still combined with the objects that are named. Among these rhymes is the following :—

One old Oxford ox opening oysters ;
Two teetotums totally tired of trying to trot to Tad-
    bury ;
Three tall tigers tippling tenpenny tea ;
Four fat friars fanning fainting flies ;

And so on to

Twelve typographical typographers typically translat-
    ing types.   (1846, p. 111.)

Other rhymes of this kind depend for their
consistency on alliteration only, such as :—

Robert Rowley rolled a round roll round,
A round roll Robert Rowley rolled round ;
Where rolled the round roll Robert Rowley rolled
    round.   (1842, p. 128.)

Robert Rowley is perhaps a name for thunder,
since a rhyme recited in the North of England as
a charm against thunder is :—

Rowley, Rowley, Rattley-bags ;
Take the lasses and leave the lads.

            (1876, p. 15.)

Another rhyme of this class begins :—

Peter Piper picked a peck of pickled pepper, etc.

            (1842, p. 129.)

And the time-honoured rhyme, " When a
twister a twisting," etc., has been traced back by

Halliwell to a collection of 1674.   This has a French parallel :—

> Si un cordonnier accordant veut accorder sa corde,
>   etc.

I do not know if the English or the French version is the older one.

CHAPTER XIII

CHANTS OF THE CREED

THE game of *Twelve Days*, especially in one French version, shows that instruction was conveyed by the cumulative mode of recitation. There are many pieces enlarging on matters of belief—Hebrew, Christian, Druidical, and heathen—which in the same way associate numbers with objects. The comparison of these pieces suggests that they are all derived from one original source. They may fitly be termed Chants of the Creed.

One of these cumulative chants is included in the Hebrew service for the night of the Passover, which is called *Echod mi jodea*, "He who knows."[1] It is recited to a monotonous tune after the return of the family from celebration, either by

---

[1] Tylor, E. B., *Primitive Culture*, I, 87, citing Mendes, *Service for the First Nights of the Passover*, 1862.

the master of the house or by the assembled company. The dialogue form, I am told, is no longer observed. The piece begins :—

> Who knoweth One?—I, saith Israel, know One.
> One is God, who is over heaven and earth.
> Who knoweth Two?—I, saith Israel, know Two.
> Two tables of the covenant; but One is our God who is over the heavens and the earth . . ."

And so forth to the last verse, which is as follows :—

> Who knoweth thirteen?—I, saith Israel, know thirteen : Thirteen divine attributes—twelve tribes—eleven stars—ten commandments—nine months preceding childbirth—eight days preceding circumcision—seven days of the week—six books of the Mishnah—five books of the Law—four matrons—three patriarchs—two tables of the covenant—but One is our God, who is over the heavens and the earth.

The same chant adapted to matters of Christian belief, but carried only from one to twelve, is current also in Latin, Italian, Spanish, French, German, and Danish. Among ourselves it is set as a song. But the objects which are associated with the numbers are not uniformly the same, and this renders it probable that the chants were composed independently of one another. This view is supported by the fact that some of the items that are named in the Christian chants are not Christian, and are, in fact, identical with the items named in the entirely heathen chants.

The Latin version of the Chant of the Creed has been traced back to the second half of the sixteenth century. Its words were set to music in a motet for thirteen voices by Theodor Clinius (d. 1602), a Venetian by birth (E., p. 408). Another Latin version of the chant goes back to 1650. The chant begins :—

Dic mihi quid unus?
—Unus est Jesus Christus [*or* Deus] qui regnat in aeternum [*or* coelis]. (A., I, 420.)

"Tell me, what is One? One is Jesus Christ [*or* God] who reigns in eternity [*or* in heaven]."

The answers further explain two as the testaments, three as the patriarchs, four as the evangelists, five as the books of Moses, six as the water-jugs of Cana in Galilee, seven as the gifts of the spirit (*or* the candelabra lit before God), eight as the beatitudes, nine as the orders (*or* choirs of the angels), ten as the commandments, eleven as the disciples (*or* stars seen by Joseph),

L

twelve as the articles of the faith (*or* the apostles).

The Chant of the Creed as recited in Spain (A., II, 142) is set in the same form, and explains the numbers in much the same manner, except that six are the days of the Creation, and eleven are eleven thousand virgins. Another version (A., II, 104) associates the Virgin with one, the three Maries with three, while nine, like the Hebrew chant, indicates the months of expectancy of the Virgin. In a Portuguese version also, nine are the months of Christ's becoming, and eleven are eleven thousand virgins (A., II, 102).

Throughout Italy and in Sicily the Chant of the Creed is known as *Le dodici parole della Verità*, "the twelve words of truth." They are generally put into the lips of the popular saint, Nicolas of Bari, who is said to have defeated the evil intentions of Satan by teaching them. These Italian chants for the most part agree with the Latin chant already cited, except that two in the Abruzzi is associated with the sun and the moon ; five is explained as the wounds of Jesus *or* of St. Francis, and eleven stands for the articles of the Catholic faith (A., I, 419; II, 97).

In Denmark the Chant of the Creed is put into the lips of St. Simeon, and begins :—

> Stat op, Sante Simeon, og sig mig, hvad een er?
> "Stand forth, St. Simeon, and tell me, what is one."

The explanations in this case are strictly Christian, Jesus Christ standing for One. The souls saved by God from the ark (*sjaele frelste Gud udi Arken*) stand for eight (Gt., II, 68).

In Languedoc also the chant is current in a Christian adaptation which agrees with the Latin, except that the Trinity stands for three ; the wounds of Jesus, as in the Italian chant, stand for five ; the lights in the temple stand for six ; and the joys of our Lady stand for seven (M. L., p. 478).

From Europe the Chant of the Creed has been carried to Canada, where a version is sung in French to a monotonous tune in four beats at a formal kind of dance, called a *ronde religieuse*—a religious round. To this dance six couples stand up ; each dancer represents a number. To the sound of their singing they move in a chain, each person turning first to the right, then to the left. When number six is reached in singing, and every time that six recurs in the chant, the dancing stops, and to the words "*six urnes de vin remplies*," the dancers who represent even numbers turn first to the right, then to the left, and make a deep bow, while those that represent uneven numbers perform the same ceremony the other way about (G., p. 298). Then the dancing is resumed. This figure, judging from the description, exactly corresponds to the Grand Chain in Lancers, except that six couples dance instead of four or eight.

In the Canadian chant the explanations of the numbers are all Christian, except that for eleven they say eleven thousand virgins, which agrees with the virgins of the Spanish and Portuguese chants. These eleven thousand virgins are mentioned also in a version of the chant current in Zürich, which, unlike the others, carries the numbers to fifteen. It enumerates Christian matters similar to those already named as far as nine choirs of angels, and further associates ten with thousands of knights, eleven with thousands of virgins, the apostles with twelve, the disciples with thirteen, the helpers in need (*Nothelfer*) with fourteen, the mysteries with fifteen. This chant is set in the old way of question and answer, and the answers are recited in cumulative form (R., p. 268).

The Chant of the Creed in a late development is preserved in the form of a religious poem among ourselves which is called *A New Dyall*. Two versions of it are preserved in the MS. Harleian 5937, which dates from about the year 1625. They have been printed by F. S. A. Sandys among his *Christmas Carols*. The refrain of the one recalls the celebration of Twelve Days :—

> In those twelve days, in those twelve days, let us be
>   glad,
> For God of His power hath all things made.

In both pieces the dialogue form is dropped, and there is no attempt at cumulation.

> One God, one baptism, and one faith,
> One truth there is the Scripture saith ;

Two Testaments, the old and new,
We do acknowledge to be true;
Three persons are in Trinity,
Which make one God in Unity;
Four sweet evangelists there are
Christ's birth, life, death, which do declare;
Five senses like five kings, maintain
In every man a several reign;
Six days to labour is not wrong,
For God Himself did work so long;
Seven liberal arts has God sent down
With divine skill man's soul to crown;
Eight in Noah's ark alive were found,
When (in a word) the World lay drowned.
Nine Muses (like the heaven's nine spheres)
With sacred tunes entice our ears;
Ten statutes God to Moses gave
Which, kept or broke, do spoil or save;
Eleven with Christ in heaven do dwell,
The twelfth for ever burns in hell;
Twelve are attending on God's Son;
Twelve make our Creed, " the dyall's done." [1]

The objects named in this poem agree in most
cases with those of the Latin chant, but six, there
associated with the water-jugs in Cana of Galilee,
is here associated with the days of the Creation,
which correspond with the six days of the Creation
of the Spanish Chant of the Creed, and with the
six working days of the week of a heathen dia-

[1] Sandys, F. S. A. : *Christmas Carols*, p. 59 ff.

logue story to which we shall return later. The number eight is here associated with the persons saved in the ark of Noah, as in the Chant of the Creed which is current in Denmark.

CHAPTER XIV

HEATHEN CHANTS OF THE CREED

W E now turn to those versions of the Chant of the Creed which are heathen in character. Again we have versions before us in the vernacular of Brittany, Spain, Scotland, and several set in the form of songs that are current in different parts of England.

The most meaningful and elaborate versions of the chant come from Brittany. One is called *Les vêpres des grenouilles*. It is set in the form of instruction, and begins :—

> Can caer, Killoré. Iolic, petra faot dide?
> Caera traïc a gement orizoud ti.   (L., I, p. 95.)

" Chant well, Killore. Iolic, what shall I sing?—The most beautiful thing thou knowest."

And it enumerates, " One silver ring to Mary, two silver rings, three queens in a palace, four acolytes, five black cows, six brothers and six sisters, seven days and seven moons, eight beaters of the air, nine armed sons, ten ships on the shore, eleven sows, twelve small swords." This combination of objects with numbers from one to twelve agrees most closely with the enumeration of the game of *Twelve Days*.

The longer version of the Breton chant was interpreted by its editor as a chant of instruction, and he claimed for it a Druidical origin. It begins :—

Beautiful child of the Druid, answer me right well.
—What would'st thou that I should sing?—
Sing to me the series of number one, that I may learn it this very day.
—There is no series for one, for One is Necessity alone, the father of death, there is nothing before and nothing after.

And we read of two as oxen yoked to a cart; of three as the beginning, the middle, and the end of the world for man and for the oak; also of the three kingdoms of Merlin; of four as the stones of Merlin for sharpening the swords of the brave; of five as the terrestrial zones, the divisions of time, the rocks on one sister (*sic*); of six as babes of wax quickened into life through the power of the moon; of seven as the suns, the moons, and the planets, including *La Poule* (i.e. the constellation of Charles's Wain; of eight as the winds that blow, eight fires with the great fire lighted in the month of May on the War Mountain; of nine as little white hands near the tower of Lezarmeur, and as maidens who groan; of nine also as maidens who dance with flowers in their hair and in white robes around the well by the light of the moon; 'the wild sow and her young at the entrance to their lair, are snorting and snarling, snarling and snorting; little one, little one, hurry to the apple-tree, the wild boar will instruct you'; of ten as the enemy's boats on the way from Nantes, 'woe to you, woe to you, men of Vannes'; of eleven as priests 'coming from Vannes with broken swords and blood-stained garments, and crutches of hazel-wood, of three hundred only these eleven ones are left'; of twelve as months and signs, 'Sagittarius, the one before the last, lets fly his pointed arrow. The twelve signs are at war. The black cow with a white star on her forehead rushes from the forest (*des despouillés*) pierced by a pointed arrow, her blood flows, she bellows with raised head. The trumpet sounds, fire and thunder, rain and wind. No more, no more, there is no further series.' (H. V., p. 1.)

The contents of this chant in several particulars agree with the shorter one. Seven stands for days, eight for winds, and ten for boats.

A similar chant comes from Spain, which gives the answers with a curious variation. For in this case most of the numbers are explained as one less of one kind and one more of another. Thus one stands for the Wheel of Fortune; two for one clock and bell; three for the handle of a mortar (? *la mano del almiles*); four for three basins and one dish; five for three jars of red wine and two of white (*or* for the wounds of St. Francis); six for the loves you hold (*amores que teneis*); seven for six cassocks and a cape; eight for seven butchers and one sheep; nine for eight hounds and one hare; ten for the toes; eleven for ten horsemen and one leader (*breva*, ?acorn); twelve are probably pigs.

Exactly as in the other chants the numbers

are set in question and answer, the answer being
in cumulative form :—

> Quién me dirá que no es una ?—
> La rued de la fortuna.   (Ma., p. 68.)

"Who will tell me what is one ?—One is the Wheel of
Fortune," and so forth.

In this Spanish version there is the alternative
of associating five with the jars of wine of Cana
or with the wounds of St. Francis, both of which
are Christian conceptions that occur in the Christian chants—the wounds of St. Francis in the
Italian chant, and the jugs of wine, six in
number, in the chant as it is sung and danced
in Canada.   Christian conceptions are also introduced into some of the numerous versions of the
heathen Chants of the Creed that are current
among ourselves, but they are relatively few, and
by their nature suggest a change from heathen
to Christian matters of belief.

The oldest version of this chant was printed
by Chambers from an unpublished collection of
songs by P. Buchan.   It is in dialogue form,
and, as in the case of the Druidical chants, its

words indicate a teacher who is instructing his
pupils :—

    1. We will a' gae sing, boys,
       Where will we begin, boys ?
       We'll begin the way we should,
       And we'll begin at ane, boys.

       O, what will be our ane, boys?
       O, what will be our ane, boys?
       —My only ane she walks alane,
       And evermair has dune, boys.

    2. Now we will a' gae sing, boys ;
       Where will we begin, boys?
       We'll begin where we left aff,
       And we'll begin at twa, boys.

       What will be our twa, boys?
       —'Twa's the lily and the rose
       That shine baith red and green, boys.
       My only ane she walks alane,
       And evermair has dune, boys.

    3. Now we will a' gae sing, boys, . . . etc.
       What will be our three, boys?
       Three, three thrivers. . . . etc.
                             (1870, p. 44.)

Four's the gospel-makers, five's the hymnlers o' my
bower, six the echoing waters, seven's the stars in heaven,
eight's the table rangers, nine's the muses of Parnassus,
ten's the commandments, eleven's maidens in a dance,
twelve's the twelve apostles.

Further variations of this chant have been recovered in Dorsetshire, Cornwall, Derbyshire, Norfolk, and elsewhere. Many of them at the close of each line insert the interjection *O* in the place of the word *boys*. This drew the suggestion from Dr. Jessopp that the song was connected with the so-called *Seven great Os*, a song sung at vespers during Advent before the *Magnificat* from 16 December to Christmas Eve. It took its name from the first line in the song, which begins *O Sapientia*.

The Dorsetshire version is still sung at Eton, and is known as "Green grow the rushes oh," the words that form the chorus :—

> Solo :   I'll sing you one oh !
> Chorus :   Green grow the rushes oh !
>   What is your one oh ?
> Solo :   One is one and all alone
>   And ever more shall be so.[1]

The same order is observed for the next verse, the soloist explaining two, the chorus adding one, and so forth. In this version we have two lily-white boys, three rivals, four gospel makers, five symbols at your door, six proud walkers, seven

[1] Byrne, S. R., *Camp Choruses*, 1891, p. 91.

stars in the sky, eight bold rainers, nine bright
shiners, ten commandments, eleven for the eleven
that went up to heaven, twelve for the twelve
apostles.

A Chant of the Creed is sung in Cornwall by
the sailors, and begins :—

> Come and I will sing you !
> —What will you sing me ?
> I will sing you one, oh !
> —What is your one, oh !
> Your one is all alone,
> And ever must remain so.

The explanations which follow are very cor-
rupt. Two are lily-white maids clothed all in
green, oh !; three are bright shiners; four are
gospel-makers; five are the ferrymen in a boat
and one of them a stranger; six is the cheerful
waiter; seven are the stars in the sky; eight are
the archangels; nine are the bold rainers; ten
are the commandments; eleven went up to heaven;
twelve are the apostles.[1]

In Derbyshire the chant is associated with the
harvest festival, and takes the form of a drinking

[1] Lang, A., "At the Sign of the Ship," in *The Gentleman's Magazine*, January, 1889, p. 328.

song. It begins with three, but the explanations of one and two are preserved in the last verse, in which the song is carried back to its real beginning :—

Plenty of ale to-night, my boys, and then I will sing you.
What will you sing?—I'll sing you three oh.
What is the three O? . . .

The last verse enumerates:—Twelve apostles; eleven archangels; ten commandments; nine bright shiners; eight, the Gabriel riders; seven golden stars in heaven; six came on the board; five by water; four Gospel rhymers; three threble thribers; two lily-white maids and one was dressed in green O.[1]

This version of the chant was sung or recited at harvest-time in Norfolk also, and began :—

A : I'll sing the one O.
B : What means the one O?
A : When the one is left alone, No more can be seen O !
C : I'll sing the two Os.
D : What means the two Os?

Two's the lily-white boys—three's the rare O—four's the gospel makers—five's the thimble in the bowl—six is the provokers—seven's the seven stars in the sky—eight

[1] Addy, S. O., "Two Relics of English Paganism," in *The Gentleman's Magazine*, July, 1890, p. 46.

is the bright walkers—nine's the gable rangers—ten's the ten commandments—'leven's the 'leven evangelists—twelve's the twelve apostles.[1]

The version current in Herefordshire is preserved as far as number eight only :—

Eight was the crooked straight,
Seven was the bride of heaven,
Six was the crucifix,
Five was the man alive,
Four was the lady's bower [*or* lady bird, *or* lady, *or* lady's birth ?],
Three was the Trinity,
Two was the Jewry,
One was God to the righteous man
To save our souls to rest. Amen.[2]

Some of our nursery rhymes which are non-sensical represent these lines in a further degradation :—

One, two, three, four, five,
I caught a hare alive ;
Six, seven, eight, nine, ten,
I let her go again. (*c.* 1783, p. 48.)

And the following, in which " sticks " takes the

[1] Jessopp, " A Song in Arcady," in *Longman's Magazine,* June, 1889, p. 187.
[2] From Stoke Prior, Herefordshire, in Addy, S. O., *Household Tales and Traditional Remains,* 1895, p. 150.

M

place of *crucifix*, while "straight" recalls *crooked straight* :—

> One, two, buckle my shoe,
> Three, four, shut the door,
> Five six, pick up sticks,
> Seven, eight, lay them straight. (1810, p. 30).

The rhyme is sometimes continued as far as twenty :—

> Nine, ten, a good fat hen,
> Eleven, twelve, who shall delve ? *etc.*

The tabulation of the explanations of numbers of these various songs will give an idea of the degradation to which words are liable, when they have lost their meaning. It shows also that some information can be recovered from comparing what is apparently nonsensical.

One.—Scotland : One all alone.
    Dorset : One is one and all alone.
    Cornwall : Is all alone and ever must remain so.
    Derbyshire : One was dressed in green O.
    Norfolk : One left alone no more can be seen O.
    Hereford : One was God to the righteous man.

Two.—Sc. : Lilly and rose.
    Dt. : Lilly white boys.
    C. : Lilly white maids clothed in green.
    Db. : Lilly white maids.
    N. : Lily white boys.
    H. : Jewry.

Three.—Sc. : Thrivers.
        Dt. : Rivals.
        C. : Bright shiners.
        Db. : Threble thribers.
        N. : Rare O.
        H. : Trinity.

Four.—Sc. : Gospelmakers.
        Dt.   ,,
        C.   ,,
        Db. : Gospelrhymers.
        N. : Gospelmakers.
        H. : Lady's bower.

Five.—Sc. : Hymnlers of my bower.
        Dt. : Symbols at your door.
        C. : Ferrymen in a boat and one a stranger.
        Db. : By water.
        N. : Thimble in a bowl.
        H. : Man alive.

Six.—Sc. : Echoing waters.
        Dt. : Proud walkers.
        C. : Cheerful waiter.
        Db. : Came on board.
        N. : Provokers.
        H. : Crucifix.

Seven.—Sc. : Stars in heaven.
        Dt. : Stars in the sky.
        C.   ,,   ,,
        Db. : Golden stars.
        N. : Stars in the sky.
        H. : Bride of heaven.

Eight.—Sc. : Table rangers.
      Dt. : Bold rainers.
      C. : Archangels.
      Db. : Gabriel riders.
      N. : Bright walkers.
      H. : Crooked straight.

Nine.—Sc. : Muses.
      Dt. : Bright shiners.
      C. : Bold rainers.
      Db. : Bright shiners.
      N. : Gable rangers.

Ten.—Sc. : Commandments.
      Dt.   ,,
      C.   ,,
      Db.   ,,
      N.   ,,

Eleven.—Sc. : Maidens in a dance.
      Dt. : Went up to heaven.
      C.   ,,   ,,
      Db. : Archangels.
      N. : Evangelists.

Twelve.—Sc. : Apostles.
      Dt.   ,,
      C.   ,,
      Db.   ,,
      N.   ,,

From this table we see that the *thrivers* of Scotland are *threble thribers* in Derbyshire. These, according to the explanation of Addy, are the three

Norns or white ladies,[1] and this view is supported by the *three queens* of the one Breton chant, which probably suggested *The Three Maries* of the one Spanish version.

Again, the *table rangers* of the Scottish song are *Gabriel riders*, otherwise known as *Gabriel hounds* or *gabbe ratches* in Derbyshire. *Gabriel hounds* is a word applied to the winds. The winds are also associated with eight in the one Breton chant. In Cornwall *bright shiners* are associated with three, but in Dorsetshire and Derbyshire *bright shiners* are associated with nine, and nine is the number of maidens in one Breton chant also. We are reminded of the priestesses who were devoted to religious rites on some island of the Atlantic, perhaps Ushant, off Brittany, when Pytheas, in the fourth century before Christ, visited these shores. Nine of them attended a famous oracle, and professed to control the weather.

The interest of these chants is increased when we compare them with what folk-lore preserves on the subject. The followers of Mohammed

[1] Addy, S. O., loc. cit., p. 150.

tell a tale which describes how a rich man promised a poor man his ox if he could explain to him the numbers, and the following dialogue ensued :—

What is one and not two?—God is one.
What is two and not three?—Day and night [*or* the sun and the moon].

And further : three for divorces from one's wife ; four for the Divine books (i.e. the Old and New Testament, the Psalter and the Koran); five for the states of Islam ; six for the realms in Nizam ; seven for the heavens that surround the throne of God (A., II, 230).

The same story in a more primitive form is told in Ditmarschen, a district bordering on Holstein, in which also the numbers are carried to seven only. But in this case a peasant's property stood forfeited to the "little man in grey," unless he found an explanation to the numbers. He despaired of doing so, when Christ intervened and instructed him as follows :—

One stands for wheelbarrow ; two stands for a cart ; three for a trivet ; four for a waggon ; five stands for the fingers of the hand ; six for the working days of the week ; seven for the stars of the Great Bear.   And the peasant remained in the possession of his goods (R., p. 137).

More primitive still is the story as told in Little Russia.   In this case a man bartered away his soul for six pigs.   After three years the devil came to fetch him.   But the devil was met by an old, old man who successfully cheated him of his due.   The dialogue between them was : " Who is in the house ?—One and not one (that is two). And how about two ?—It is well to thrash two at a time.   It is well to travel three at a time.   He who has four has a waggon.   He who has five sons has company.   Six pigs the devil had, but he left them with a poor man, and now he has lost them for ever " (A., II, 227).

The comparison of these stories with the Chants of the Creed shows that the dialogue stories are older in contents, and probably in form also, than the cumulative pieces.   In both, superhuman power is conveyed by associating numbers with objects.   This power in the dialogue pieces is attributed to the " little man in grey " of the German piece, who may be intended

for Death, and to the devil in the Russian piece.
In the pieces where numbers are associated with
Christian articles of belief, the superhuman power
is attributed to a popular saint, viz. St. Simeon
in Denmark and St. Nicholas in Italy, who make
use of their power to overcome Satan.

The dialogue stories explain the numbers only
as far as six or seven. This in itself indicates
that they are relatively early. Some of the explanations they contain reappear in the cumulative
Chants of the Creed, both in their Christian
and in their heathen variations. Thus the " one
wheel" of the wheelbarrow in the German dialogue story, reappears as the Wheel of Fortune
in the Spanish chant, and as the " One that walks
alone" of the Scottish chant. Perhaps this idea
underlies the one O, or circle of our late English
songs also. Two in the dialogue story is explained as a cart; one Breton Chant of the Creed
associates two with an ox-cart also. In the
Mohammedan dialogue story two is explained as
the sun and moon, and this explanation reappears
in the Christian chant as sung in the Abruzzi.
Six, which the German dialogue story explains as

the working days of the week, has the same meaning in our song of the *New Dyall*.   Seven, which
the German dialogue story associates with the constellation of Charles's Wain, reappears as *La
Poule* in the Breton Chant of the Creed, as seven
bright shiners in our English songs, and as the
stars seen by Joseph in the Latin Chant.

These points of likeness cannot be due to mere
chance; they indicate a relationship between all
the pieces which associate objects with numbers.
There has been some discussion as to which
Chant of the Creed has the greater claim to
priority—whether the Breton was based on the
Christian, or the Christian on the Hebrew, and
how these stand in relation to the various heathen
chants.   But the analysis of these pieces renders
it probable that they are all derived from an
earlier prototype, and this prototype is perhaps
to be sought in the dialogue stories.   For in the
Chants of the Creed the explanations of the
numbers are often abstract in meaning, whereas
in the dialogue pieces they are simple objects,
mostly wheels or circles, which may well have
appeared magical in themselves to the primitive

mind.   Again, the purpose of the Chants of the Creed is to convey religious instruction as a protection against the devil, while in the dialogue stories in the last instance the theme is the acquisition of pigs, and pigs were esteemed valuable possessions from a remote period of antiquity.

CHAPTER XV

SACRIFICIAL HUNTING

M ANY nursery rhymes and pieces relate to sacrificial hunting. This hunting goes back to the time when certain animals were looked upon as tabu in that they were generally held in reverence, and ill-luck befell him who wittingly or unwittingly did them harm. At the same time one animal of the kind was periodically slain. It was actually killed, but its spirit was held to be incarnate in other creatures of its kind, and it therefore continued to be spoken of as alive.

The custom of killing the divine animal belongs to an early stage of social evolution, since it stands in no relation to agriculture, and perhaps took rise before men tilled the soil. The animal that was slaughtered was generally looked upon as the representative of a certain clan, or as

171

constituting the bond between a number of kinsmen.[1]

Among the creatures that were sacrificially hunted in different parts of Western Europe were a number of small birds. Many of our nursery pieces relate to the hunting of the wren. A peculiar importance was attached to this bird from a remote period in antiquity, possibly on account of the golden crest worn by one kind of these birds. This importance was expressed by the term "little king." In Greek the wren was $\beta \alpha \sigma \iota \lambda \iota \sigma \kappa o \varsigma$, in Latin he was *regulus* or *rex avium*. In France he is *roitelet*; in Italy he is *reatino*; in Spain he is *reyezuolo*; in Germany he is *zaunkönig*; in Wales he is *bren*, a word allied to our wren. The sacrifice of a bird that was so highly esteemed, must have a deeper significance. Possibly his sacrifice was accepted in the place of the periodical sacrifice of the real king, a primitive custom which dates far back in history. If so, the practice of slaying the wren represents the custom of killing the king "of the woods" at a later stage of development.

[1] Frazer, J. G., *The Golden Bough*, 1900, II, 442 ff.

The designation of king as applied to the wren naturally called for an explanation. It was accounted for by the story according to which the birds challenged one another as to who could fly highest. The eagle flew higher than the other birds, but the diminutive wren hid beneath his wing, and, being carried up by the eagle, started on his own flight when the eagle tired, and so proved his superiority (Ro., II, 293). The story dates from the period when cunning was esteemed higher than brute force, and when cheating was accepted as a legitimate way of showing one's powers. Among the fairy tales of Grimm one tells how the wren, whose young had been spoken of disrespectfully by the bear, challenged the four-footed beasts of the forest, and by a similar strategem proved his superiority over them also (No. 152). Thus the kingship of the wren extended to the four-footed as well as to the feathered tribes.

The lines that celebrate the *Hunting of the Wren* are included in several of the oldest nursery collections. They depend for their consistency on repetition; there is no attempt at cumulation.

In the collection of 1744 the piece stands as
follows :—

I

We will go to the wood, says Robbin to Bobbin,
We will go to the wood, says Richard to Robbin,
We will go to the wood, says John and alone,
We will go to the wood, says everyone.

II

We will shoot at a wren, says Robbin to Bobbin,
We will shoot at a wren, says Richard to Robbin, etc.

III

She's down, she's down, says Robbin to Bobbin, etc.

IV

How shall we get her home, says Robbin to Bobbin, etc.

V

We will hire a cart, says Robbin to Bobbin, etc.

VI

Then hoist, hoist, says Robbin to Bobbin, etc.

VII

She's up, she's up, says Robbin to Bobbin, etc.

In the collection of 1783 there is an additional
verse :—

So they brought her away after each pluck'd a feather,
And when they got home shar'd the booty together.

(c. 1783, p. 20.)

Another version of this chant from Scotland is included in Herd's collection of songs, which goes back to 1776.[1] In this the wren "is slayed," "conveyed home in carts and horse," and is got in by "driving down the door cheeks." The characters in this case are Fozie Mozie, Johnie Rednosie, Foslin 'ene, and brethren and kin. The song ends:—

VIII

> I'll hae a wing, quo' Fozie Mozie,
> I'll hae anither, quo' Johnie Rednosie,
> I'll hae a leg, quo' Foslin 'ene,
> And I'll hae another, quo' brither and kin.

In the toy-book literature of the eighteenth century I have come across the expression, "They sang the Fuzzy Muzzy chorus," which may be related to these names.

Another variation of the chant sung in Carmarthenshire[2] is set in the form of a dialogue, and the fact is insisted on that the hunt shall be carried out in the old way in preference to the new:—

[1] Herd, David, *Ancient and Modern Scottish Songs*, reprint, 1869, II, 210.

[2] Mason, M. H., *Nursery Rhymes and Country Songs*, 1877, p. 47.

I

O, where are you going, says Milder to Malder,
O, I cannot tell, says Festel to Fose,
We're going to the woods, says John the Red Nose,
We're going to the woods, says John the Red Nose.

II

O, what will you do there? says Milder to Malder . . .
| We'll shoot the Cutty Wren, says John the Red Nose. |

III

O, how will you shoot her . . .
| With cannons and guns, *etc.* |

IV

O, that will not do . . .
| With arrows and bows, *etc.* |

V

O, how will you bring her home . . .
| On four strong men's shoulders, *etc.* |

VI

O, that will not do . . .
| In waggons and carts, *etc.* |

VII

O, what will you cut her up with? . . .
| With knives and forks, *etc.* |

VIII

O, that will not do . . .
| With hatchets and cleavers, *etc.* |

IX

O, how will you boil her? . . .
| In kettles and pots, *etc.* |

X

O, that will not do . . .
| In cauldrons and pans, *etc.* |

XI

O, who'll have the spare ribs, says Milder to Malder,
O, I cannot tell, says Festel to Fose,
We'll give them to the poor, says John the Red Nose,
We'll give them to the poor, says John the Red Nose.

Further variations of the chant have been recovered from the Isle of Man and from Ireland,
where the hunt is kept up to this day.   In the
Isle of Man it used to take place on 24 December,
though afterwards on St. Stephen's Day, that is
27 December, which according to the old reckon-
ing was the beginning of the New Year.[1]   On this
day people left the church at midnight and then
engaged in hunting the wren.   When the bird
was secured, it was fastened to a long pole with
its wings extended, and it was carried about in
procession to the singing of the chant :—

We hunted the wren for Robin the Bobbin.

[1] Waldron, *Description of the Isle of Man*, reprint 1865,
p. 49 ; also Train, T., *History of the Isle of Man*, 1845, II,
126.

N

This chant further describes that the bird was hunted with sticks and stones, a cart was hired, he was brought home, he was boiled in the brewery-pan, he was eaten with knives and forks, the king and the queen dined at the feast, and the pluck went to the poor.

The behaviour of the huntsmen was not, however, in keeping with these words; for the bearers of the wren, after making the circuit, laid it on a bier and carried it to the parish churchyard, where it was buried with the utmost solemnity, and dirges were sung over it in the Manx language, which were called the knell of the wren. The company then formed a circle outside the churchyard and danced to music.

In the middle of the nineteenth century the wren was still hunted in the Isle of Man and was carried by boys from door to door, suspended by the legs in the centre of two hoops. These crossed each other at right angles and were decorated with evergreens and ribbons. The boys recited the chant. In return for a coin they gave a feather of the wren, so that before the end of

the day the bird hung featherless. A super-
stitious value was attached to these feathers, for
the possession of one of them was considered an
effective preservative from shipwreck during the
coming year among the sailors. At this time the
bird was no longer buried in the churchyard, but
on the seashore or in some waste place.

The hunt in the Isle of Man was accounted for
by the legend that in former times a fairy of
uncommon beauty exerted such influence over
the male population of the island that she
induced them by her sweet voice to follow her
footsteps, till by degrees she led them into the sea,
where they perished. At last a knight-errant
sprang up, who laid a plot for her destruction,
which she escaped at the last moment by taking
the form of a wren. But a spell was cast upon
her by which she was condemned on every
succeeding New Year's Day to reanimate the
same form, with the definite sentence that she
must ultimately perish by human hand. In this
form the legend is told by Train. Waldron
relates the same story, which explained why the
female sex are now held of little account in the

island, but the fairy according to him was transformed into a bat.

In Ireland also the wren was generally hunted during the eighteenth century, and continues to be hunted in Leinster and in Connaught, but I have come across no chant of the hunt. The bird was slain by the peasants, and was carried about hung by the leg inside two crossed hoops, and a custom rhyme was sung which began :—

> The wren, the wren, the king of all birds,
> Was caught St. Stephen's Day in the furze ;
> Although he's little, his family's great,
> Then pray, gentlefolks, give him a treat.

(1849, p. 166.)

The bird was slain, but it was not therefore dead. This is conveyed by the tale told in the Isle of Man, and by the following custom observed in Pembrokeshire on 6 January, that is on Twelfth Day. On this day one or several wrens were secured in a small house or cage, sometimes the stable lantern, which was decorated with ribbons and carried from house to house while the following lines were sung :—

Joy, health, love, and peace,
Be to you in this place.
By your leave we will sing
Concerning *our king :*
Our king is well drest,
In silks of the best,
With his ribbons so rare
No king can compare.
In his coach he does ride
With a great deal of pride
And with *four footmen*
To wait upon him.
We were four at watch,
And all nigh of a match ;
And with powder and ball
We fired at his hall.
We have travell'd many miles,
Over hedges and stiles,
To find you this king
Which we now to you bring.
Now Christmas is past,
Twelfth Day is the last.
Th' Old Year bids adieu ;
Great joy to the new.   (1876, p. 35.)

On grouping together these various pieces, we
are struck by their likeness, and by the antiquity
of their allusions. The bird was usually slain
with stones and sticks, which are among the most
primitive weapons. In Wales *bows and arrows*,
which are old also, were declared preferable to

cannons and guns. In Wales the bird was cut up
with *hatchets and cleavers* in preference to *knives
and forks;* it was boiled in the *brewery pan*, or in
cauldrons and pans, in preference to *kettles and
pots;* and it was conveyed about in a *waggon or
cart* in preference to being *carried on four men's
shoulders.* Sometimes the bird was plucked.
Finally it was cut up in a sacrificial manner ; one
wing—another—one leg—another—and the spare
ribs or the pluck, as the least valuable part of the
feast, went to the poor.

The representative huntsmen in England are
Robbin, Bobbin, Richard, and John-all-alone.
In Scotland they are Fozie-Mozie, Johnie Rednosie, and Foslin, besides "the brethren and
kin." In Wales they are Milder, Malder, Festel,
Fose, and John the Rednose. Of these characters
only Robin and Bobbin (the names are sometimes
run together) and Richard, reappear in other
nursery pieces. In the oldest collection of 1744
stand the lines :—

> Robbin and Bobbin, two great belly'd men,
> They ate more victuals than three-score men.

(1744, p. 25.)

These powers of eating perhaps refer to the first share of these characters at the feast. They are further dwelt on in the following nursery rhyme :—

> Robin the Bobbin, the big-headed hen [or ben]
> He eat more meat than four-score men.
> He eat a cow, he eat a calf,
> He eat a butcher and a half ;·
> He eat a church, he eat a steeple,
> He eat the priest and all the people.
>
> (c. 1783, p. 43.)

To which some collections add :—

> And yet he complained that his belly was not full.

Other pieces dilate on Robin and Richard as lazy in starting, and on Robin, whose efforts as a huntsman were attended with ill luck :—

> Robin and Richard were two pretty men,
> They lay in bed till the clock struck ten :
> Then up starts Robin, and looks at the sky,
> Oh ! brother Richard, the sun's very high.
> You go before, with the bottle and bag,
> And I will come after, on little Jack Nag.
>
> (c. 1783, p. 42.)

> Robin-a-Bobbin bent his bow,
> Shot at a woodcock and killed a yowe [ewe] ;
> The yowe cried ba, and he ran away,
> And never came back till Midsummer day.
>
> (1890, p. 346.)

Halliwell saw a relation between the huntsman of this verse and the bird robin, since the robin was reckoned to disappear at Christmas and not to return till Midsummer. As a matter of fact, the robin leaves the abodes of man and retires into the woodland as soon as the sharp winter frost is over.   However this may be, the presence of the wren and of the robin was mutually exclusive, as we shall see in the pieces which deal with the proposed union, the jealousy, and the death of these two birds.

CHAPTER XVI

BIRD SACRIFICE

THE custom of slaying the wren is wide-spread in France also. But the chants that deal with it dwell, not like ours, on the actual hunt, but on the sacrificial plucking and dividing up of the bird. Moreover, the French chants depend for their consistency not on repetition like ours, but are set in cumulative form. Both in contents and in form they seem to represent the same idea in a later development.

At Entraigues, in Vaucluse, men and boys hunted the wren on Christmas Eve, and when they caught a bird alive they gave it to the priest, who set it free in church. At Mirabeau the hunted bird was blessed by the priest, and the curious detail is preserved that if the first bird was secured by a woman, this gave the sex the right to jeer at and insult the men, and to blacken their faces with mud and soot if they caught them. At Carcassonne, on the first Sunday of December, the young people who dwelt in the street of Saint-Jean went out of the town armed with sticks and stones to engage in the hunt. The first person who struck the bird was hailed king, and carried the bird home in procession. On the last of December he was solemnly introduced to his office as king; on Twelfth Day he attended mass in church, and then, crowned and girt about with a cloak, he visited the various dignitaries of the place, including the bishop and the mayor, in a procession of mock solemnity. This was done as late as 1819.[1] This identification of the bird and the men explains the hiring of a cart or waggon to convey " the bird " in our own custom-rhymes.

The Breton chant on " plucking the wren," *Plumer le roitelet* begins :—

> Nin' ziblus bec al laouenanic
> Rac henès a zo bihanic | *bis.*   (L., I, p. 72.)

" We will pluck the beak of the wren, for he is very small," and continues, " We will pluck the left eye of the wren, for he is very small "

[1] Rolland, loc. cit., II, 295 ff.; Frazer, loc. cit., II, 445 ff.

and then enumerates right eye, left ear, right ear, head, neck, chest, back, belly, left wing, right wing, left buttock, right buttock, left thigh, right thigh, left leg, right leg, left foot, right foot, first claw of left foot and every claw in succession of this and of the other foot. The last sentence is "We will pluck the tail of the wren," and then sentence after sentence is repeated to the first, "We will pluck the beak of the wren because he is very small, we have plucked him altogether."

Another poem preserved in Breton relates how the wren was caught and caged and fed till the butcher and his comrades came and slew it, when the revelry began (L., I, p. 7).

I have often wondered at the cruel sport of confining singing birds in cages. Possibly this goes back to a custom of fattening a victim that was sacrificially slain. For the wren is tabu in Brittany as among ourselves, and in popular belief the nestlings of each brood assemble with the parent birds in the nest on Twelfth Night, and must on no account be disturbed. This reflects the belief that the creature that is slain during the winter solstice, at its close starts on a new lease of life.

The wren is not the only bird that was sacrificially eaten in France, judging from the chants that are recorded. A chant on "plucking the lark," *Plumer l'alouette*, is current in the north of France which begins :—

> Nous la plumerons, l'alouette,
> Nous la plumerons, tout de long.

(D. B., p. 124.)

"We will pluck the lark, we will pluck it altogether."

And it enumerates the bird's beak, eyes, head, throat, back, wings, tail, legs, feet, claws.

A variation of the same chant is sung in Languedoc, where it is called *L'alouette plumée*, "the plucked lark," and is described as a game (M. L., p. 457).

Again, the dividing up of the thrush forms the subject of a chant which is sung in Brittany in the north (L., I, p. 81), and in Languedoc in the south. It is called *Dépecer le merle*, and preserves the further peculiarity that the bird, although

it is divided up, persists in singing. The version
current in Languedoc begins :—

Le merle n'a perdut le bec, le merle n'a perdut le bec,
Comment fra-t-il, le merle, comment pourra-t-il chanter?
Emai encaro canto, le pauvre merle, merle,
Emai encaro canto, le pauvre merlatou.

(M. L., p. 458.)

"The thrush has lost his beak, how will he manage to
sing, and yet he sings, the poor thrush, yet he goes on
singing."

The chant then enumerates the bird's tongue,
one eye, two eyes, head, neck, one wing, two
wings, one foot, two feet, body, back, feathers,
tail; always returning to the statement that
the bird, although it is divided up, persists in
singing.

The French word *merle* stands both for thrush
and for blackbird. The blackbird is held in
reverence among ourselves in Salop and Mont-
gomeryshire, and blackbird-pie was eaten in
Cornwall on Twelfth Night.[1] But there is no
reference to the sacrificial slaying of the bird, as
far as I am aware. In the French chant the

[1] Thomas, N. W., "Animal Superstitions" in *Folk-Lore*,
September, 1900, p. 227.

bird continues to sing although it is killed.   The same idea finds expression in our nursery song of *Sing a Song of Sixpence*.   This piece, taken in conjunction with the eating of blackbird-pie in Cornwall and the French chants, seems to preserve the remembrance of the ancient bird sacrifice.   The first verse of this rhyme appears in the collection of 1744, in which "naughty boys" stands for blackbirds.   In other collections the piece runs as follows :—

> Sing a song of sixpence, a bagful of rye,
> Four and twenty blackbirds baked in a pye
> And when the pye was open'd, the birds began to sing ;
> Was not this a dainty dish to set before the king?
> The king was in his parlour counting out his money,
> The queen was in the kitchen eating bread and honey,
> The maid was in the garden hanging out the clothes,
> Up came a magpie and bit off her nose.
>
> (*c.* 1783, p. 26.)

The magpie is "a little blackbird" in the version of Halliwell, which continues :—

> Jenny was so mad, she didn't know what to do,
> She put her finger in her ear and cracked it right in two.

Halliwell (1842, p. 62) noted that in the book called *Empulario or the Italian Banquet* of 1589,

there is a receipt " to make pies so that the birds
may be alive in them and fly out when it is cut
up," a mere device, live birds being introduced
after the pie is made. One cannot but wonder if
the device was a mere sport of fancy, or if it
originated from the desire to give substance to an
ancient belief.

Again, the robin redbreast was sacrificially
eaten in France at Le Charme, Loiret, on
Candlemas, that is on February the first (Ro., II,
264). There are no chants on the sacrifice of
the robin in France, as far as I know. Among
ourselves, on the other hand, where no hunting of
the robin is recorded, a piece printed both by
Herd [1] and Chambers suggests his sacrifice. The
piece is called by Chambers *The Robin's Testament,*and it describes how the bird, on the approach
of death, made a bequest of his several parts,
which he enumerated exactly in the way of the
sacrificial bird-chants current in France. They
were his neb, feathers of his neb, right leg, other
leg, feathers of his tail, and feathers of his
breast, to each of which he attributed a mystic

[1] Herd, David, loc. cit., II, 166.

significance.   The piece in the combined versions
stands as follows :—

> Guid-day now, bonnie Robin
> How lang have you been here?
> I've been bird about this bush,
> This mair than twenty year !

> *Chorus :* Teetle ell ell, teetle ell ell.
> Tee, tee, tee, tee, tee, tee, tee,
> Tee, tee, tee, teetle eldie.

> But now I am the sickest bird
> That ever sat on brier ;
> And I wad make my testament,
> Guidman, if ye wad hear.

> " Gar tak this bonnie *neb* o' mine,
> That picks upon the corn,
> And gie 't to the Duke o' Hamilton
> To be a hunting horn.

> " Gar tak these bonnie feathers o' mine,
> *The feathers o' my neb,*
> And gie to the Lady o' Hamilton
> To fill a feather-bed.

> " Gar tak this guid *right leg* o' mine
> And mend the brig o' Tay ;
> It will be a post and pillar guid,
> It will neither ban nor gae.

> " And tak this *other leg* o' mine
> And mend the brig o'er Weir ;
> It will be a post and pillar guid,
> It 'll neither ban nor steer.

(Herd only).

" Gar tak these bonnie feathers o' mine
    The feathers o' my tail,
And gie to the Lady o' Hamilton
    To be a barn-flail.

" Gar tak these bonnie feathers o' mine
    The *feathers o' my breast,*
And gie to ony bonnie lad
    That 'll bring me to a priest."

Now in there came my Lady Wren
    With mony a sigh and groan ;
"O what care I for a' the lads
    If my wee lad be gone ? "

Then robin turned him round about
    E'en like a little king,
"Go, pack ye out at my chamber door,
    Ye little cutty quean."

(Chambers only).

Robin made his testament
    Upon a coll of hay
And by came a greedy gled
    And snapt him a' away.   (1870, p. 40.)

The Robin's Testament should be compared with
the French piece called *Le Testament de l'Ane,*
" the testament of the ass," of which a number
of variations have been collected.   The "testament
of the ass " was recited outside the church on the

o

so-called *Fête de l'Ane*, "the feast of the ass," which was kept in many cities of France till a comparatively recent date. In Douai it was celebrated as late as the year 1668. On this occasion an ass was brought into church, and an office was recited in Latin, which enlarged on the ass that carried the Holy Family into Egypt, the ass which bore Christ into Jerusalem, the ass of Balaam, and so forth. Its chorus consisted of braying, in which the assembled canons joined. This service in church was preceded by a recitation outside the holy edifice, which was in the vernacular, and which, in dialogue form, enlarged on the several parts of the ass.[1]

One of these dialogue pieces, current in Franche-Comté, describes how the she-ass, conscious of the approach of death, bequeathed her feet and ears to her son, her skin to the drummer, her tail to the priest to make an aspergill, and her hole to the notary to make an inkpot (B., p. 61).

---

[1] Clémént, Madame, *Histoire des fêtes civiles et religieuses du Nord*, 1834, p. 184. Also, Du Cange, Glossarium, *Festum Asinorum*.

Another version, at greater length, is in the form of instruction which is given by the priest to the child, whose answers are set in cumulative form.

" The feast of the ass," in the words of Bujeaud, " must have been very popular, since I have often heard the children of Angoumais and Poitou recite the following piece " :—

Le prêtre : Que signifient les deux oreilles de l'âne ?
L'enfant : Les deux oreilles de l'âne signifient les deux grands saints, patrons de notre ville.
Le prêtre : Que signifie la tête de l'âne ?
L'enfant : La tête de l'âne signifie la grosse cloche et la langue fait le battant de cette grosse cloche qui est dans le clocher de la cathédrale des saints patrons de notre ville. (B. I., p. 65.)

" The priest : What do the ears of the ass stand for ?— The child : The ears of the ass stand for the two great patron saints of our city.—The priest : What does the head stand for ?—The head stands for the great bell, and the tongue for the clapper of the great bell which is in the belfry of the cathedral of the holy saints, the patrons of our city."

We then read of the throat which stands for the entrance to the cathedral—the body for the cathedral itself—the four legs, its pillars—the heart and liver, its great lamps—the belly, its alms-box—the tail which stands for the aspergill

—the hide which stands for the cope of the priest —and the hole which stands for the holy-water stoup.

This chant on the parts of the ass is among the most curious survivals. At first one feels inclined to look upon it as intended to convey ridicule, but this idea is precluded by the existence of *The Robin's Testament*, and by the numerous pieces which enumerate the several parts of the bird in connection with the bird sacrifice. Again in this case we are led to look upon the piece as a garbled survival of some heathen form of ritual. The ass, however, was not known in Western Europe till a comparatively late period in history. It has no common Aryan name, and the question therefore arises how it can have come to be associated with what is obviously a a heathen form of ritual.

Mannhardt, with regard to German folk-lore, pointed out that the ass was substituted in many places for the hare, which was tabu, and with which it shared the peculiarity of having long ears. This substitution was favoured by their likeness of name: *heselín, heselken*. (M., p. 412.)

We are led to inquire if the ass in Western Europe can have taken the place of another animal also, and we find ourselves confronted with the following facts:—

Dicky among ourselves is applied to a bird, especially to a caged (? perhaps a sacrificial) bird; the word Dicky is also widely applied to an ass, properly to a he-ass.[1] The ass is often called by nicknames exactly like the small wild birds: Jack-ass, Betty-ass, Jenny-ass, in form closely correspond to Jack-daw, Magpie, and Jenny Wren of the feathered tribe. The word Jack-ass moreover is applied both to the four-footed beast and to a member of the feathered tribe. Nicknames probably originated in the desire to conceal a creature's true identity.

In Scotland the word *cuddy* again stands both for an ass and for some kinds of bird, including the hedge-sparrow and the moor-hen.[1] The word cuddy is said to be short for Cuthbert, but it seems to be related also to cutty, an adjective applied to the wren (cf. above, p. 176, 193), the derivation and meaning of which are uncertain.

[1] Murray's Dictionary : *Dicky, cuddy, ass, Jackass.*

The same overlapping of terms exists in France, where the ass is popularly called Martin (Ro., IV, 206, 223, 233), while the feathered martins include the *martin pêcheur*, kingfisher, the *martin rose*, goatsucker, and the *martinets* (Ro., II, p. 70). In Germany also, where no bird-chants are recorded, as far as I am aware, the expression *Martinsvogel* is applied to a bird of augury of uncertain identity, sometimes to the redbreast (Gr., p. 946). And a current proverb has it, *Es ist mehr als ein Esel der Martin heisst*, "he is more than an ass who is called Martin." (Ro., IV, 233.) In Barmen boys parade the streets on the eve of St. Martin's Day, asking for contributions, and, if they receive nothing, they sing :—

Mäten ist ein Esel, der zieht die Kuh am Besel.

(B., p. 363.)

"Martin is an ass, he pulls the cow by the tail," that is, "he has no money in his purse."

These various survivals support the view that the ass in Western Europe somehow got mixed up with the birds. When and how this came about is difficult to tell. The representatives of Christianity were in a position to accept the feast of the ass, since the ass figured largely in the Old and the New Testaments. But we do not know if they consciously did so, and introduced the ass in the place of another animal, or if they took over an animal which had before their time been accepted in the place of a bird.

CHAPTER XVII

THE ROBIN AND THE WREN

ONE side of the subject remains to be discussed. It is the relation of the robin to the wren. Many custom rhymes, legends, and nursery pieces name the birds together, and they sometimes enlarge on the jealousy of the birds, and on the fact that their presence was reckoned mutually exclusive. Perhaps the birds, looked at from one point of view, were accounted the representatives of the seasons, and, as such, came and went by turns.

The robin and the wren are mentioned together in several custom rhymes, some of which mention other birds also :—

> The robin redbreast and the wren
> Are God's cock and hen. (1826, p. 292.)

In Warwickshire they say :—

The robin and the wren
Are God Almighty's cock and hen ;
The martin and the swallow
Are God Almighty's bow and arrow.

(1870, p. 188.)

In Lancashire this takes the form :—

The robin and the wren are God's cock and hen ;
The spink and the sparrow are the de'il's bow and arrow.

(1892, p. 275.)

This association of the sparrow with the bow
and arrow reappears in some nursery pieces, as
we shall see later.

The robin and the wren are coupled together
also in the following rhyme from Scotland, which
has found its way into some modern English
nursery collections :—

The robin redbreast and the wran
Coost out about the parritch pan ;
And ere the robin got a spune
The wran she had the parritch dune.

(1870, p. 188.)

The Robin's Testament already quoted concludes with anger on the part of the robin
at the entrance of the wren, whose appearance
heralds his death.   Other pieces describe the

inverse case, when the wren dies in spite of the robin's efforts to keep her alive. This conception forms the subject of a Scottish ballad called *The Birds' Lamentation*, which is included in the collection of David Herd of the year 1776. It contains the following lines:—

The Wren she lyes in Care's bed, in meikle dule and
 pyne, O !
Quhen in came Robin Red-breast wi' sugar saps and wine,
 O !
—Now, maiden will ye taste o' this?—It's sugar saps and
 wine, O !
Na, ne'er a drap, Robin, (I wis); gin it be ne'er so fine,
 O !
—Ye're no sae kind's ye was yestreen, or sair I hae mis-
 tae'n, O !
Ye're no the lass, to pit me by, and bid me gang my
 lane, O !
And quhere's the ring that I gied ye, ye little cutty
 quean, O !
—I gied it till an ox-ee [tomtit], a kind sweat-heart o'
 myne, O !

The same incidents are related of real birds in the toy-book called *The Life and Death of Jenny Wren*, which was published by Evans in 1813 " for the use of young ladies and gentlemen :—

A very small book at a very small charge,
To teach them to read before they grow large."

The story begins :—

Jenny Wren fell sick upon a merry time,
In came Robin Redbreast and brought her sops and wine ;
Eat well of the sop, Jenny, drink well of the wine.
Thank you Robin kindly, you shall be mine.

The wren recovered for a time, but her behaviour was such as to rouse the robin's jealousy.
She finally died, and the book concludes with the
lines :—

Poor Robin long for Jenny grieves,
At last he covered her with leaves.
Yet near the place a mournful lay
For Jenny Wren sings every day.

It was an ancient superstition that the robin
took charge of the dead, especially of those who
died by inadvertence.

The proposed union of the robin and the wren
forms the subject also of a story that was taken
down from the recitation of Mrs. Begg, the sister
of the poet Burns. She was under the impression
that her brother invented it. It describes how
the robin started on Yule morning to sing before
the king, and of the dangers, in the form of
Poussie Baudrons, of the grey greedy gled, of
Tod Lowrie, and of others, he encountered by the

way. He sang before the king and queen, who gave him the wee wren to wed. Then he flew away and sat on a briar (1870, p. 60). There is no sequel.

In all these stories the wren is described not as a cock-bird, but as a hen-bird, which is incompatible with the idea of kingship that is expressed by the bird-chants. Perhaps the idea of the kingship is the older one. For in the legend told in the Isle of Man as an explanation of the custom of killing the wren, this bird is described as a fairy, that is, of the female sex, and legends that are intended to account for a custom are necessarily of a more recent date than the custom which they explain. The wren in Normandy also is sometimes spoken of as a hen-bird, *La poulette du bon Dieu*, God Almighty's hen. One custom-rhyme current in Scotland directly associates the bird with the Lady of Heaven :—

> Malisons, Malisons, mair than tens,
> That harry the Ladye of Heaven's hen.
>
> (1870, p. 186.)

There is another toy-book relating the proposed union of the robin and the wren, which leads up to the death of the robin.   It is called *The Courtship, Marriage, and Picnic Dinner of Cock Robin and Jenny Wren*, and was first issued by Harris in 1810.   In this book other animals took part in the ceremony.   The cock blew the horn, the parson rook carried Mother Hubbard's book, the lark sang, the linnet, the bullfinch, and the blackbird all officiated.   A picnic dinner followed, to which the raven brought walnuts, the dog Tray brought a bone, the owl brought a sack of wheat, the pigeon brought tares, and so forth.   The enjoyment was at it height—

When in came the cuckoo and made a great rout,
He caught hold of Jenny and pulled her about.
Cock robin was angry and so was the sparrow,
Who now is preparing his bow and his arrow.
His aim then he took, but he took it not right,
His skill was not good, or he shot in a fright,
For the cuckoo he missed, but cock robin he killed,
And all the birds mourned that his blood was so spilled.

The cuckoo, it will be remembered, was the bird of the god Thor, and the enemy of matrimonial bliss.

This story of a bird-wedding does not stand alone.   From France and Spain come a number

of pieces which similarly describe the proposed
wedding of birds and end in disaster. In Languedoc one is called *Lou mariage de l'alouseta*,
" the wedding of the lark." It begins :—

> Lou pinson et l'alouseta
> Se ne voulien maridà.   (M. L., p. 490.)

"The spink (*or* finch) and the lark intended to
marry. On the first day of the wedding they had
nothing to eat."

A gadfly on his neck brought a loaf, a gnat
brought a cask, a butterfly a joint, and a sparrow
brought grapes. The flea jumped out of the bed
and began to dance, and the louse came forth
from the rags and seized the flea by the arm.
Then the rat came out of his hole and acted as
drummer, when in rushed the cat and devoured
him.

Exactly the same story is told in much the same
form in Catalan of *La golondrina y el pinzon*, "The
goldfinch and the swallow," but the verses on the
gay rat and the destructive cat are wanting (Mi.,
p. 398). Other versions have been recorded in the
centre and in the North of France, one of which
was printed in 1780 (Ro., II, 180, 212; D. B.,

p. 106). From thence the song was probably carried to Canada, where it reappears as *Pinson et Cendrouille*, "The finch and the nuthatch" (G., p. 275). Here the ending is that the rat played the fiddle, and the cat rushed in and spoilt the fun.

These stories of bird-weddings should be compared with one which describes how the flea and the louse combined to set up house together and came to grief. It is told in Catalan of *La purga y er piejo* (Ma., p. 74). In Languedoc the same story is told of *La fourmiho e le pouzouil*, "the ant and the flea" (M. L., p. 508). In form these pieces closely correspond with our bird-wedding. There is the same communal feast to which the various guests bring contributions, and the same revelry which ends in disaster.

This Spanish piece on the housekeeping of the louse and the flea has a further parallel in the story called *Laüschen und Flöhchen*, "The louse and the flea," which is included in the fairy tales of Grimm (No. 30). But the German story is told in the cumulative form of recitation, and its contents are yet one stage more primitive. There is nothing on a wedding celebration. The louse and the flea set up house together, and began by brewing beer in an eggshell. The flea fell in by inadvertence and was drowned. Then the louse set up the wail. In this the door joined by jarring, the broom by sweeping, the cart by running, the dungheap by reeking, the tree by shaking, till they were all carried away by the brook.

Much the same story, told in cumulative form also and equally primitive, is current among ourselves. It seems to be old (1890, p. 454), and is called *Tittymouse and Tattymouse*. We read how Tittymouse and Tattymouse went a-leasing (gleaning), and set about boiling a pudding. Titty fell in and was scalded to death. Then Tatty set up the wail. It was joined by the stool that hopped, the besom that swept, the window that creaked, the tree that shed its leaves, the bird that moulted its feathers, and the girl that spilt the milk. Finally an old man fell from a ladder, and all were buried beneath the ruins. Tittymouse and Tattymouse are usually represented as mice, but the word tittymouse is also allied to titmouse, a bird. Titty and Tatty are among the many rhyming compounds of which the meaning is no longer clear.

The conceptions on which these pieces are based all recall primitive customs. The wedding is a communal feast to which contributions of different kinds are brought by the several guests. Again the death of one individual draws that of a number of others in its wake. On comparing these various pieces, we find that those which are set in cumulative form, judging from their contents, are the more primitive. This supports the view that the cumulative form of recitation represents an earlier development in literature than rhymed verse.

The toy-book on *The Courtship of Cock Robin and Jenny Wren* attributes the robin's death to the carelessness of the sparrow. The sparrow is also described as causing the death of the robin in the knell of the robin, which is one of our oldest and most finished nursery pieces. The death of the robin is a calamity, his blood is treasured, he is buried with solemnity. In the collections of 1744 and 1771 the knell stands as follows : —

P

1. Who did kill Cock Robbin?
    I said the sparrow, with my bow and arrow,
    And I did kill Cock Robbin.

2. Who did see him die?
    I said the fly, with my little eye,
    And I did see him die.

3. And who did catch his blood?
    I said the fish, with my little dish,
    And I did catch his blood.

4. And who did make his shroud?
    I said the beetle, with my little needle,
    And I did make his shroud.

The Death and Burial of Cock Robin formed
the contents of a toy-book that was printed by
Marshall in London, by Rusher in Banbury, and
others.   One of the early toy-books belonging to
Pearson, which are exhibited at South Kensington
Museum, contain verses of this knell with quaint
illustrations.   The toy-book published by Marshall which contains the knell, is described as
" a pretty gilded toy, for either girl or boy."
It leads up to the knell by the following verse,
which occurs already as a separate rhyme in the
nursery collection of 1744 :—

Little Robin Redbreast sitting on [*or* sat upon] a pole,
   Niddle noddle [*or* wiggle waggle] went his head [tail]
And poop went his hole.

This is followed by the picture of a dead robin with the words :—

> Here lies Cock Robin, dead and cold,
> His end this book will soon unfold.

We then read the four verses of the knell already cited, and further verses on the owl so brave that dug the grave; the parson rook who read the book; the lark who said amen like a clerk; the kite who came in the night; the wren, both cock and hen; the thrush sitting in a bush; the bull who the bell did pull.

In another toy-book the magpie takes the place of the fly, and from the illustration in a third one we gather that not a bull but a bullfinch originally pulled the bell.

The toy-book published by Marshall concludes :—

> All the birds of the air
> Fell to sighing and sobbing,
> When they heard the bell toll
> For poor Cock Robin.

(Reprint 1849, p. 169 ff.)

The antiquity of this knell of the robin is apparent when we come to compare it with its foreign parallels, which are current in France,

Italy, and Spain. In these rhymes also, those who undertake the office of burial are usually birds, but the nature of him whose death is deplored remains obscure.

In Germany he is sometimes *Sporbrod*, sometimes *Ohnebrod*, that is "breadless" (Sim., p. 70), a term which may indicate a pauper. The piece current in Mecklenburg is simpler in form than ours.

> Wer is dod?—Sporbrod.
> Wenn ehr ward begraben?
> Oewermorgen abend, mit schüffeln un spaden,
> Kukuk is de kulengräver,
> Adebor is de klokkentreder,
> Kiwitt is de schäüler,
> Mit all sin schwester un bräüder. (W., p. 20.)

"Who is dead?—Breadless. When will he be buried? —On the eve of the day after to-morrow, with spades and with shovels. The Cuckoo is the gravedigger, the Stork is the bell-ringer, the Pee-wit acts as scholar, with all his sisters and brothers."

The knell that is recited in Languedoc is called *Las Campanas*, the bells. One version begins:—

> Balalin, balalan, La campana de Sant Jan
> Quau la sona? Quau la dis?—Lou curat de Sant-Denis.
> Quau sona lous classes?—Lous quatre courpatrasses.
> Quau porta la caissa?—Lou cat ambe sa maissa.
> Quau porta lon doù?—Lou pèirou.[1]
>
> [1] (M. L., p. 225.)

"Ding dong, the bell of St. John.—Who tolls it and who says (mass) ?—The priest of St. Denis.—Who sounds the knell?—The four ravens.—Who bears the coffin?—The cat in its maw.—Who wears mourning?—The partridge."

Another version preserves the trait that the individual's possessions took part in the mourning:

"Balanli, balanlau, the bells near Yssingeaux are all tolled through April. Who is dead?—Jan of the Gardens (dos Ort). Who carries him to his grave?—His great coat. Who follows him?—His hat. Who mourns for him?—The frog. Who sings for him?—The toad. Who forsakes him?—His sabots. Who says so?—Jan the less. What shall we give him?—The legs of a dog. Where shall we find them?—Near Chalencons there are plenty. (M. L., p. 232.)

Jan dos Ort in other versions of the knell is called *Jean le Porc*, also *le père du jardin*; and in the latter case, *le père petit*, the little father, pronounces him dead, and receives dogflesh (M. L., pp. 226, 230).

The Italian knell is quite short :—

Who is dead?—Beccatorto.

Who sounds the knell?—That rascal of a punch.

(Quel birbon de pulcinella, Ma., p. 133.)

The Spanish knell is not much longer :—

? Quién s' ha muerto.—Juan el tuerto.
? Quién lo llora.—La señora.
? Quién lo canta.—Su garganta.
? Quién lo chilla.—La chiquilla. (Ma., p. 62.)

" Who is dead?—Crooked Juan. Who mourns for him?
—The swallow. Who sings for him?—His coat. Who
calls for him?—The quail."

Victor Smith, with reference to these chants,
enlarged on the possible nature of Jan, or Juan,
of the French and Spanish versions, who is called
also " the father of the gardens," and who was
given dogflesh to eat. In illustration he adduced
the legend of the god Pan, who was looked upon as
the father of gardens, and who was supposed to
eat dogflesh (M. L., p. 227). Dogs were sacrificed at the Lupercalia which were kept in April,
and the month of April is actually mentioned in
one of the French chants. If this interpretation
is correct, the knells on Jan current in France
and Spain preserve the remembrance, not of a bird
sacrifice, but of a dog sacrifice. But the Italian
name Beccatorto is probably ⌐rossbill (R., II, 160),
and birds appear as the chief mourners in most
of the foreign chants, as they do in ours.

CHAPTER XVIII

CONCLUDING REMARKS

I N conclusion it seems well to glance back over the ground that has been traversed, and to consider what information can be gleaned from the comparative study of nursery rhymes.

At the outset we saw that our nursery collections consist of a variety of pieces of diverse origin. Many rhymes are songs or snatches of songs which have no direct claim on the attention of the student of folk-lore. Other pieces are relatively new, although they contain names that are old. Thus, Old King Cole and Mother Hubbard are names that go some way back in history ; the story of the woman who fell asleep out of doors and forgot her identity, preserves an old tradition ; Jack and Jill are connected with Scandinavian mythology ; while Tommy Linn, the hero of several nursery pieces, figures in romantic ballad literature also.

A more primitive form of literature is represented by traditional dancing and singing games, to which many nursery rhymes can be traced. These games in several instances preserve the remains of celebrations that date from heathen times. In the last instance they survive as a diversion of the ballroom. Incidental allusions enabled us to establish the relation between the Cotillon, the Cushion Dance, and the game of *Sally Waters*. This latter game preserves features of a marriage rite, which was presided over by a woman who was addressed as mother. The words used in the game and the rite suggest that there may be some connection between the game of *Sally Waters* and the name of Sul, the local goddess of the waters at Bath.

Other traits preserved in the games of *The Lady of the Land*, *Little Dog I call you*, and *Drop Handkerchief*, probably date from the same period. For the comparison of these games with their foreign parallels enabled us to realize that, in their case also, it is a question of a presiding mother, who, in some of the German versions of the game, was addressed by the name of a heathen mother divinity. *Engelland*, that is Babyland, and the disabled condition of the human mother, which are mentioned in these games, reappear in the ladybird rhymes. In these we also come across Ann or Nan, who reappears under the same name in the corresponding rhymes of Switzerland and Swabia.

On comparing our rhymes with those of other countries, we find that the same thoughts and conceptions are usually expressed in different countries in the same form of verse. The words that are used, both in England and abroad, in dancing and singing games, in custom rhymes like those addressed to the ladybird, and in riddle-rhymes such as that in *Humpty-Dumpty*, are set in short verse that depends on tail rhyme for its consistency. Distinct from them are the pieces that depend for their consistency on repetition and cumulation. Some of these are obviously intended to convey instruction, like the chants of Numbers and of the Creed. Others appear to be connected with the making and unmaking of spells. Again in this case, the parallel pieces of different countries are set in the same form of verse.

Another class of rhymes is represented by the chants on bird sacrifice. Those current among ourselves depend for their consistency on repetition only, while those current abroad which present details on the plucking and the dividing up of the bird, are related in cumulative form. Perhaps the repetition which preserves the simpler facts of the custom is the older form of recitation. The kingship of the wren which is accepted throughout Europe, and which dates some way back in history, in some of these chants is connected with the kingship of the man who was engaged in the hunt. Possibly the custom of killing the king was overlaid by the custom of sacrificing a bird in his stead.

The reverence felt for the wren is equalled among ourselves by the reverence felt for the robin, whose knell remains one of our finest, and perhaps one of our oldest nursery pieces. It is set in dialogue form, which seems to have been generally associated with bells, but which was a

primitive manner of recitation, as we gather
from other pieces.

The information which can be derived from
nursery rhymes corroborates what has been
collected elsewhere concerning different stages of
social history in the heathen past.   Some pieces
preserve allusions which carry us back to customs
that prevailed during the so-called mother age;
others, quite distinct from them, are based on
conceptions that may have taken rise before man
tilled the soil.   The spread of European nursery
rhymes, taken in the bulk, appears to be in-
dependent of the usual racial divisions.   Some of
our rhymes, such as that of the ladybird and
Humpty Dumpty have their closest parallels in
Germany and Scandinavia; others, such as the
bird-chants and the animal weddings, have corresponding versions in France and in Spain.   Moreover, some of the ideas that are expressed in
rhymes carry us beyond the confines of Europe.
The chafer was associated with the sun in Egypt,
the broken egg engaged the attention of the
thinking in Tibet.

Thus the comparative study of the nursery

rhymes of different countries throws light on allusions which otherwise remain obscure, and opens up a new vista of research. The evidence which is here deduced from some rhymes, and the interpretation put on others, may be called into question. Much remains to be said on the subject. But the reader will, I think, agree that nursery rhymes preserve much that is meaningful in itself, and worth the attention of the student.

LIST OF FOREIGN COLLECTIONS

THE following foreign collections are referred to by initials in the text :—

A. Archivio Storico per lo Studio delle tradizione popolari. Articles by Canizzaro, I, 1882; by Wesselowski, II, 1883, *etc.*

Br. *Birlinger :* Nimm mich mit, 1871.

Bo. *Boehme, F. M. :* Geschichte des Tanzes, 1884.

B. *Bujeaud, I. :* Chants et chansons des provinces de l'Ouest, 1895.

C. P. Corpus Poet. Borealium, ed. Vigfusson and Powell, 1883.

D. *Dumersan, M. :* Chansons et rondes enfantines, 1856.

Du. *Dunger, H. :* Kinderlieder aus dem Vogtland, 1874.

D. B. *Durieux et Bruyelles :* Chants et chansons du Cambrésis, 1864.

E. *Erk, L. :* Deutscher Liederhort, 1856.

F. *Frischbier, H. :* Preussische Volksreime und Spiele, 1867.

G. *Gagnon, E. :* Chansons pop. du Canada, 1865.

Gr. *Grimm, J. :* Deutsche Mythologie, reprint 1875.

Gt. *Grundtvig :* Gamle Danske Minder, 1854-6.

H. *Handelmann :* Volks — und Kinderspiele aus Schleswig Holstein, 1862.

H. V.	*Hersart de la Villemarqué :* Barzas Breis, 1867.
L.	*Luzel, F. M.:* Chansons de la Basse Bretagne, 1890.
M.	*Mannhardt :* Germanische Mythen, 1858.
Ma.	*Marin, Rodriguez :* Rimas Infantiles, 1882.
Me.	*Meier, Ernst :* Kinderreime und Kinderspiele aus Schwaben, 1851.
Mi.	*Mila y Fontanals:* Romancerillo Catalan, 1882.
Mo.	*Morlidas :* Grande Encyclopedie des Jeux.
M. L.	*Montel et Lambert :* Chants populaires du Languedoc, 1880.
N.	*Newell, W. W.:* Songs of American Children, 1884.
N. & Q.	Notes and Queries.
R.	*Rochholz:* Alemannisches Kinderlied und Spiel, 1859.
Ro.	*Rolland :* Faune populaire, 1876–83.
S.	*Schleicher :* Volksthümliches aus Sonneberg, 1858.
Sch.	*Schuster, F. W.:* Siebenbürg-sächs. Volkslieder, 1856.
Sim.	*Simrock :* Das deutsche Kinderbuch.
St.	*Stöber :* Elsässisches Volksbüchlein, 1842.
V.	*Vernaleken:* Spiele und Reime aus Oesterreich, 1873.
W.	*Wossidlo :* Volksthümliches aus Mecklenburg, 1885.

ALPHABETICAL INDEX

Q